About the Author

S. Job, born in 1963, worked as a teacher and a civil servant from 1987 to 2012. *Tracing a Lost City* (a travelogue, 2020), *Elephas Estate* (a novel, 2020), and *Rain on Taro Leaf* (a collection of haiku, 2022) are his previously published works. He lives in Kochi, India.

First Rain

S. Job

First Rain

Olympia Publishers
London

www.olympiapublishers.com
OLYMPIA PAPERBACK EDITION

Copyright © S. Job 2024

The right of S. Job to be identified as author of
this work has been asserted in accordance with sections 77 and 78 of
the Copyright, Designs and Patents Act 1988.

All Rights Reserved

No reproduction, copy or transmission of this publication
may be made without written permission.
No paragraph of this publication may be reproduced,
copied or transmitted save with the written permission of the publisher,
or in accordance with the provisions
of the Copyright Act 1956 (as amended).

Any person who commits any unauthorised act in relation to
this publication may be liable to criminal
prosecution and civil claims for damage.

A CIP catalogue record for this title is
available from the British Library.

ISBN: 978-1-80439-644-5

This is a work of fiction.
Names, characters, places and incidents originate from the writer's
imagination. Any resemblance to actual persons, living or dead, is
purely coincidental.

First Published in 2024

Olympia Publishers
Tallis House
2 Tallis Street
London
EC4Y 0AB

Printed in Great Britain

Dedication

To the memory of

E. Chacko
(1937-2022)

The author's father and his first teacher of English

Acknowledgements

The author owes a debt to

Sofy

His wife, who walked him down memory lane
to places and events, thus giving him the spark
for many poems in this collection

James Houghton

Commissioning Editor, Olympia Publishers

Sálim Moizuddin Abdul Ali
(1896-1987)

Indian Ornithologist and Naturalist whose writings
have taken him to the world of birds.

Contents

RAIN

First Rain	19
Hills of Malabar Coast in May	21
Monsoon's Entry into the Malabar Coast	23
August is No Longer August in Malabar	24
Swamp After Summer Rain	26
Rain in a Banana Garden	27
Woods after a Summer Rain	28
A Rainy Dawn	30
Walking in the Rain	31
A Rainy Night	32
Rain Scenes	33
The Tongues of Rain	34
Rain is a Painter	35
An Unexpected Rain	36
Lament from an Ancient Dam	37
Swifts in a Cloudy Sky	38
Sloping Roofs of Clay Tiles	39
Seasons	41

BIRDS

Malabar Whistling Thrush	43
Koel's Melody	44
Jungle Crow	45
Barbet's Call	46

Witchery on a Windowpane 47
Junglefowl of Doddabetta 48
Jungle Babblers Confront a Rat Snake 49
Peafowl on NH766 50
Common Kingfisher 51
Wise Owl Speaks 53
Being Cormorant 54
Cormorant's Prayer 56
Nilgiri Wood Pigeon 58
White-breasted Waterhen 60
The Dance of the Peacock 61
Sparrows Attend Sunday Mass 62
A Nestling of Wagtail 63
Seven Sisters 65
Sound of Solitude 67
Junglefowl Cock 68
Malabar Parakeet 69
A White-bellied Sea Eagle Seeks a Casuarina Tree 70
Lament of the Greater Adjutant Stork 71
Silence of the Frogmouth 74
A Chat with a Taiga Flycatcher 76

WOODS

Tonight in the Dark Woods 79
Wind in the Woods 81
Shades of Green in the Woods 82
Forest Fire 83
Into the Woods 84
Commensalism 85
Jungle Safari 86
Bamboo and Wind 88

Silence of the Woods 89
Dawn in the Western Ghats 90
Yonder Hills 91
A Night Safari at Nelliyampathy 92
Forest Bathing 94
A Trek to a Montane Grassland 95

ANIMALS

Tiger Cool 98
Lion-tailed Macaque 99
Malabar Giant Squirrel of Sim's Park 101
A Baby Monkey's Tour to the Town 103
A Trunkful of Love 105
Before the Bench 106
Buffalo and Egret 109
Where a Cow is More Than a Cow 111
Spider and Cicada 114
Bears of Daroji 116
Rabid 118
A Meditating Water Buffalo 119
Jasmine and Moth 121
Hermit Crab 122

PLANTS

The Wail of a Tree 124
Indian Coral Tree 126
Memories of the Paddy Field 128
Golden Shower Tree 129
The Black Rose of Ooty's Rose Garden 130
Touch-Me-Not Plant 132
Hibiscus Flower 133

When the Coffee Garden Blooms 135

SEA

The Sea is an Artist 138
A Chat with a Crab on a Riprap 139
Memories of a Boating in Lakshadweep 141
A Thousand Seas 143
Sunset on Om Beach, Gokarna 144
A Girl Who Sells Lamps on the Beach 145
Impression 147

MAN

Alzheimer's Disease 149
A Deathbed Thought 151
That Moment 152
Creator 153
Brain and Mind 155
Fifth Candle 156
Two Brothers on a Swing 157
Onboard is General 159
Christmas Night 160
The Last Day in Office 161
Toddy Tapper 163
Pearl Anniversary 165
Wake 167
Smell the Roses 169
Adieu, Alma Mater 170
Eternity 172
Onam 173
First Death Anniversary 175
O, Darling Baby, Sleep 176

Ruins of Vijayanagar	177
New Year's Day	179
To My Hilltop Hut in a Dusk	180
Missed Flowers	182
The Night Before My Wedding	184
When I Died	185
War	186
Live in the Present	187
Deaddiction Ward	188
Sundays	189
Polling Booth	190
In a Bar Near Our lady of Good Health	191
As the Earth Takes Her	192
Retrospect of a Retiree	193
Post-op	194
The Wanderer in the Town	195
Drink Responsibly	197
Birth of a Poem	198
Walking Beside a Marsh	199
Retirement Wishes	200
The Day We Left the Village	201
A Gravestone Triolet	203
A Time Seen with Ears	204
Meadow's Morning Walkers	206
Pepper Pickers of Malabar	208
Loneliness	210
The Boy Who Walked to the Skies	212
Candid Snapshots of Life	213

RAIN

First Rain

Arid April winged on thermals severe.
Thirsty were stands of trees and the hillside.
Dried up, the hills' many rivulets were
boulder beds—naked, dead reeds abound.

A rapid shift came to the mood of hills,
like a girl on a tryst keenly awaited,
when above the Malabar coast, the skies,
welcoming a cold, rain-laden wind, clapped.

Then, that evening, rain kissed the soil.
Hills bathed; with greed, soil swallowed the fall.
Washing the dirty leaves was trees' toil
in the downpour, making every twig roll.

When, with a respite to the dry spell, rain
petered, and when a dripping cuckoo plopped
onto the hedge for its wet wings to drain,
into the rain-washed April hills I stepped.

There wafted that distinct, earthy scent which,
from the pores of soil parched of summer,
only the first of rains can ever fetch—
the perfume earth keeps for rain, her lover.

The odour of wild blooms—thousands, wilted—
imbibed into earth's pores—secret rather—
now bubbles, aerosols, fragrant, gilded,
was adrift on the wet dusk—petrichor.

Hills of Malabar Coast in May

Merciless is to the hill range the May sun,
parching and fissuring shelly, its skin,
and dyeing with patches of dark brown wreaths
of dry twigs, dead, its skirts of trees and heaths.

Yellowed and dropped is lemongrass upon
boulder outcrops, warts on the hill's dry skin;
no longer stay in low warrens, rabbits,
but far uphill, still moist, in deep woods.

Where have the birds vanished, terrified by
thermals, and the reptiles, frightened by
the heatwave and have the hills hidden zones
for them and seeds to sustain till it rains?

The brooks are no longer brooks but imprints
where they stood, shed skins now of long serpents.
The bamboo groves are no longer hills' flute;
muted, they stand since the wind is silent.

The remote peaks at times shine red when down
the rocks leap tongues of fire at grasses on
cracks, spitting smoke like an engine of steam
of a hill train, spewing spirals of black brume.

The silent chains of mountains, now bone-dry,
scorched in the red-hot sun, vastly vary
from what they were years back in Malabar
in a dire shift of weather, a disaster.

Monsoon's Entry into the Malabar Coast

It was a night in the first week of June.
I woke up in the wee hours to the roar
of a wind rattling harshly, my windowpane,
clapped at by skies in a bout of thunder.

I saw silvery trails leap at sleepy
hills from a cloudy sky and trees shimmer.
From a mango tree in the yard, shady,
a fearsome owl flew in haste for shelter.

It dawned on a fabulous scene outdoors.
May's deposit of dead leaves spiralled up,
dancing gaily with the wind and the trees.
Elated, frogs croaked at the dawning's buildup.

Echoed from a distance, the sky's drumroll,
then a wail like a scream of a thousand throats.
On the trees sailed the cry, like a stern swell
of the sea, when clouds crashed as rain on the hills.

The trees went weeping in joy, and the land
drinking rain in greed. The wind played, pushing
rain that was inflicting the land a pound.
Inside dark palls, the dawn sun went hiding.

August is No Longer August in Malabar

August is no longer august in Malabar.
August's rains there, lately, go astray
like oracles on a wild dart with a sway,
forewarning the advent of times bizarre.

With this thought of August deep in my mind,
I walked into a non-stop August rain
that was staying with a fearsome campaign,
roughing up the hillside in league with the wind.

I had heard from my yard the stream downhill
roaring through rain's drum, like a trapped tiger.
What would it be like, and with that wonder,
I sloshed on the muddy hill path in the chill.

Through a rain in scream and a wind in yell,
I found my hard way down to the stream in a rage
on the banks in plunge and over the bridge
in ranting rap, throwing me in a spell.

Where stayed the bridge in the deluge, dipped,
there was a primal raft—a dead monkey;
a broken palm crown; a jackfruit, chunky;
and severed limbs of wild trees badly ripped.

Rushed in, bouncing over a rocky ridge,
a coconut, but it got stuck in the limbs
afloat, where it spun and tried many jumps,
and settled, began bobbing by the bridge.

It rained and rained and rained in drops giant;
the wind ranted and ranted in a fury.
Lost mind, a tree leapt into the stream scary.
Whined on the drowned banks, bamboos pliant.

August is no longer august in Malabar.

Swamp After Summer Rain

The earth has drunk all the water in the swamp.
In the fury of the summer sun, the marsh
went dry, and the buffaloes found it harsh
not to have the slurry of mud to clomp
through and to roll about and between spans
of grazing, they dug into the dry mud
seeking dampness. Across the bog, the wind
was but an arid draft, dribbling heat waves.

Then, with a drumroll of skies in that dusk,
lashed a summer shower, the swamp, and when
the rain slowly dropped away by dawn,
I was out for a jog by the bog, half dark.
The herd was still there but gladly standing,
dripping raindrops and watching keenly what
the rain had done to the marsh over the night
and the little pools, the grass was skirting.

Rain in a Banana Garden

The rain came with a hiss to the bananas.
Longish leaves, green—bananas' many hands—
began bouncing but soon started bending,
unable to bear the rain's brutal beating.

In the drench of rain, the farmer stood
beneath a broad banana limb that drained
rain, blinding him with streaming sheets plain.
And then the wind had a fierce campaign.

Joining the wind, throwing all their hands,
danced the bananas in thick showers.
Dancing, dancing, they went bananas. Then,
exhausted, several fell, groundward, down.

Woods after a Summer Rain

Doused were the woods from the night's flash rain,
the first in that sultry season of summer.
In the soggy peat, noisy was a croaker,
for more showers in an ardent campaign.

A cuckoo cowered on a bush for the sun
to kindle the dawn sky; it spread a wing
in quick a flick to the bush, wanting to wring
the drench of rain out of its feathers, dun.

The bog had a green snake that had a leap
to answer my footfall; it slid aside
quickly as a glistening string, green-dyed.
On I waded the bog's slippery seep.

I ran my fingers on the dark bark, damp,
pausing beside a jack tree, my beloved,
which had drunk a lot of rain; it splashed
its stock of the rain on me, saying, 'gulp'.

Grass, on its blades, had rain medals over
a clearing that had a hare out from its form.
A whirl, a dance—not leaps low—was its squirm
upon the grass that watered its fine fur.

The rain had laureled yonder rocky peak—
a white band adorning its rocky crown.
Above the rise smiled the sun from the dawn.
I wandered deep into the woods, mystique.

A Rainy Dawn

I woke up to a rainy dawn
awed by the song of the rain,
a sweet music night long that kept
me in a soothing sleep, dream-swept.

Athwart the window, I saw a
light rain kissing the yard with a
whisper and vines of devil's ivy
wearing raindrops like a white lei.

A lone bird flew out in the rain
across the gloomy sky and on
and on it soared to the weeping
sky, finally in it, melting.

The distant treeline hid in shades
of dark grey, leached from nimbus clouds
that so got purged, grew thin and ruined,
merging soon in a dark sky, bald.

The sun hardly gave a brief glimpse
from inside the raincoat of skies.
I sat to coffee, my eyes in riffle
through dawn, bathing in the drizzle.

Walking in the Rain

I love walks in the rain,
but with no umbrella,
letting the lovely rain
fully engage me, ah!

On such a walk, I hear
rain's cry of joy, lament
of pain, dismayed by fear,
sigh, and sob of regret.

Resonant is rain's cold trail
of drum and hiss and dance
with rich music, its scale
oft swayed by wind or breeze.

Rain does wipe out my tears
with its tears and showers
on me refrain that tears
my grief, my heart's showers.

A Rainy Night

Against the sidewalk, pattered the rain
and went on dancing with a gentle wind,
when dusk was approaching slowly upon
a remote hamlet and its lush back land.

Across a window, I followed the scene—
the rain was swaying, flying, diving wild
over the pavement in pale white, a sheen
when in the dusk, mellow twilight dissolved.

Popped up from nowhere, very still, an owl
on an oak tree towering beside the walk,
and beaten harshly by rain pattering still
against the path, the trees and the bleak dusk.

And then it became dark—a rainy night.
I heard a hoot from the oak, a welcome call
to a rainy, windy, gloomy, cloudy night.
The owl was very pleased—clammy nightfall.

No longer could I see the pounding rain
but I could hear it: a rooftop drumroll;
a fall from eaves; a ball on dance; a fine
meld of the wind and the rain—a rock'n'roll.

Rain Scenes

Sheets of rain obscure the distant hill range
in a delicate blue and to the rage
of the showers are he and she, drifting,
hand in hand, half-running and half-walking.

A child with a crude paper boat rushes
out of her house when the rainfall abates.
She drives to a puddle in the dooryard,
her vessel with a tiny ant onboard.

A cuckoo lost in thoughts, eluding rain
inside a hedge, discerns—rain is no bane
but a boon, and diving, it flicks water
off its wings and heads for a wet spider.

The yellow Allamanda blossoms
of the churchyard wear silvery gems—
raindrops—like the teardrops of the forlorn
weeping souls of those forever gone.

After the rain, the tall oak tree is still
in tears of joy, and the rain, like a rill,
is yet in ooze down its stark, dark trunk,
washing summer's deposits off the bark.

The Tongues of Rain

From a dream half-dreamt to the cadent drum
of dawn in the rain, I woke up from sleep.
To sad weeping eaves, like a lazy bum,
listening, I lay, relaxed, slipping deep
into my blanket and out in the yard,
howled aloud the wind, spooking mango limbs.
Across the window, I saw, fully soaked,
the enormous mango crown in a dance.
Riotous went the rain on my low roof.
Picking sounds from 'me', 'you', and 'who', it soon
fell to a lament; was the dawn-dirge proof
of pouring grief, the leitmotif of rain?

Yowling, yelling, howling, and hissing flew
furiously over the dawn, the rain.
Into its yell, I fell as a fan; who
else has as many tongues as the rain?

Rain is a Painter

Rain is a painter, rainbow a palette.
In a pale blue sky, where distant tree crowns
are apparitions, as a silhouette
rain smudges a solo bird on swift wings.

Then, pronto, with a flimsy wash of white,
she brightens up the sky and gives a tinge
verdant to the tree crowns and with a sleight
of hand works out the crowns' twiggy soft edge.

Now, she, for a time, contains her tune that
is a buzz while she is on the canvas.
She has gone somewhere, leaving her palette
that now shimmers, an arc of spectral hues.

Back is she, with a melody, this time
in soprano, her paint board now behind
she, and she with strokes in iridium
daubs on the sky, an array of clouds dimmed.

For sure, she means a background very dark.
Now, she lays over it radiant white,
a long thin stroke with a tongue like a fork.
Rain is a painter, rainbow a palette.

An Unexpected Rain

After barnstorming with a wild campaign
for about a week, retreated, the monsoon,
throwing the field back to a summer mood.
So, sans shower gear was the morning trod
of the walkers on a dirt path bisecting
a green lot, where a lazy, daydreaming
buffalo lonely lay with a reprised yawn.

The walkers walked athwart glorious dawn.
And then whined a wind, and the trees in sleep
awoke; along the walkway, dirt rolled up
like ripples; first, as one drop, next as many,
hissed in a drizzle, and leaves went weepy.
'Hey,' hooted the hikers, now helter-skelter
for a shelter that was not there anywhere.
The rain, like a cow her calf, licked the men.
The buffalo bounced up for its dear rain.

Lament from an Ancient Dam

The dam is full, and they say damn!
The rain pounds the catchment; no rein!
Stop soon; else I shall swoon, o rain!
No balm is this—no rain, a bomb.

Altar! I pray, alter this rain.
Holy terror is, wholly this pour.
Rap not, rain, and wrap no danger.
It's an old dam, cause not its ruin.

All ways downstream see you always
with fear when you daze them on days
of monsoon; know this: no man sleeps
there—sight, a site of dread, intense.

Reign the season, rain, but be kind.
The scene of you in drops is seen
with sighs of delight, but this size!
Lessen! Lesson not, rain, be kind.

Swifts in a Cloudy Sky

Along the sky are swifts in the dart,
in flight, silent, and when by cloud
in frenzied dips, lo, they go quest
for something, require they of cloud.

A flock of souls? A frantic hunt
for bodies lost in death, it missed?
Is from Elysian Fields, has it,
by these so sullen skies arrived?

And why is it in this pursuit
of bodies it forsook when dead?
The sky is in black clouds as yet;
in the rain, o souls get not soaked.

Why are you on this sojourn
this far from your peaceful abode?
From this world that inflicts deep pain,
fly back to thy asphodel field.

Sloping Roofs of Clay Tiles

To draw a house, you ask any child.
A crown will top the sketch you get.
A reversed v is that plain crest,
the roof so primal in its mind.

Certain things are aslant, like in
a lashing wind, the rain, the hills
where it touches the lower plains,
on mum's bosom, child, her violin.

The roof, I think, is meant to go slant
to drain rain and, with it, what wind
keeps on the sly and in looks, should
render a house, a crown-like crest.

But what makes me often wonder,
about earthy roofs of tiles of mud,
are times that we lived in accord—
and splendid they were—with nature.

Look at the sloping roofs peeping
the sky through an awning of trees,
bearing scars from many seasons
of rainfall but still firm roofing.

The roof of clay tiles drinks the rain
in greed in seasons of showers.
In a shoal, a croc's skin of scales
look, clay tiles, under sheets of rain.

The crocodile skin on the rooftop
is canvas primed with falling rain.
Time, an artist, often paints an
abstract painting on the rooftop.

Seasons

Is not seasons' cadence fabulous?
The winter melds one year to another,
when shortly bud, the spring's lovely flowers
which wilt on the days of sultry summer.

Then comes riding dark rain clouds, the monsoon,
whose waters quench the badly thirsty earth.
Sprout, the secret seeds in earth's dry womb, soon
to saplings, green, and grasslands go in mirth.

Once the rain is away, soon the autumn
arrives with pleasant skies and splendid crops
and slowly, it falls to the fall; for some,
the fall is autumn, which in winter drops.

Yet are erratic seasons now: warm, man,
the earth. Wither weather to no design.

BIRDS

Malabar Whistling Thrush

The dawn sun gave a wan smile to the trees.
On the leafage fell light rain, like feathers.
The horizon was sleepy, still, black-palled.
Behind brushwood, faintly, a brook mumbled.
Yet to awake to the cold dawn were the hills.
In the dooryard of my camp in the woods,
I stood eyeing an odd meld of darkness
and soft light holding the woods in vagueness.

A surreal flute flew from the dark brook.
It rose on notes to a soprano, took
a low pitch and fell in the rain's patter
to somewhat a sudden stop. A chatter
was not it, but a whistle, apparently
by a bird mimicking a song—clearly,
a melody; who else would in the brook
on the nippy dawn into music break?

The flute rose again, this time with many
singers, as if from a band through many
a song; in the background was the rain,
assisted by a cold breeze buzzing fain.
Away petered the concert in the burn
when atop the distant hills shined the sun.
On glossy blue wings up the brook, a thrush
rose, beading rain, and it was in a hush.

Koel's Melody

Koel, a cuckoo, has the call, 'coo, o…'
It calls seven times or so in one go,
rising in scale from a low-pitched 'coo, o…'
through subsequent notes to a crescendo
and at that fever pitch, it breaks off, o,
to commence it again: 'coo, o, coo, o…'
and thus, the savvy singer does bestow
summer nights, a musical gift, tempo
being the same with each set of 'coo, o.'
Only the male koel has this presto.
His love enjoys his music of 'coo, o,'
silent is she on a tall tree, though.
As I say this, stands of trees shadow
the bushes below—it's gloaming; I know
a koel shall now start its allegro.
O, it begins and pitches up pronto.
O, up goes the koel, 'coo, o, coo, o…'

Jungle Crow

If boldness takes the bird's figure, call it
jungle crow—what I feel about the crow
that on every dawn glides by my hut.

All it needs are a few moments to scout
whether, over the night, there was a kill
or whether from a nest a chick is out.

I know why it is often in a hurry.
It wants to look for tiger-kills in the woods,
where a wake of vultures is its company.

The vultures know not that it is so bold
to raid even their nests to steal the food
that as parents for their young, they hold.

Anything edible, alive or dead
is its food, cherries or berries, frog,
termites, kitchen crumbs, or crabs in mud.

It sometimes digs farmers' fertile grounds
in seasons of the harvest for groundnuts.
So, jack of all trades is it in the woods.

When the coral tree is abloom in winter,
it reaches the scarlet twigs in the dawn
with a light flick of its bill for nectar.

Barbet's Call

Harken! A 'coo', then a 'true' together
is barbet's pesky disyllabic note
from the jack tree and the hiding caller
keeps on that hideous call, incessant.

And now it dies down somewhat abruptly.
Like a green ball pelted, darts with a crack
off the jack, the barbet that, till now, hardly
contrasted with the foliage of the jack.

Of things I observe in this bird, tiny,
what amazes me the most is its fun
on moonlit nights by going whiny
all night, like filing a plaint to the moon.

Witchery on a Windowpane

Cryptic was the tap on the windowpane
that confused me every afternoon
in my humble holiday camp in the wood
and from a lazy nap, awake, I would.

I would find no one—who left soon
after tapping on the window in vain?
The rat-a-tat-tat stayed a mystery
until, one day when I saw a witchery.

A black birdie was in frantic action—
pecking at its reflection on the pane
like a smith with a hammer at the anvil.
A male robin was it from the low sill.

Junglefowl of Doddabetta

I was the last to leave Doddabetta
that evening when cried, a woods watcher,
'Time is up,'—a euphemism for 'Ah,
get out,'—and I left the peak in my car.

A Nilgiri pigeon from a bower
cooed goodbye as in quiet fell the mount.
A rhododendron waved a red flower,
wishing me a fast and safe descent.

Down a few curves, parties, many, I saw,
of junglefowl on the lonely hill road.
Alarmed by the purr of my engine, though
helter-skelter to the shoulders, they fled.

The harems in quick flights took the cover
of bushes while the cocks ran alongside
the road, throwing their necks red and amber,
and stretching out their black sickle tails wide.

As I rolled past the sickles, rearward
echoed, piercing the frigid gloaming,
the cocks' two-noted invectives uttered
rapidly—a curse indeed, harsh-sounding.

Jungle Babblers Confront a Rat Snake

From the debris of fallen leaves swiftly
rose a sisterhood of jungle babblers
in loud wrangling and on wings, it quickly
reached a coral tree rich in red flowers.

Not to nectar-rich blossoms was its flight
but to a low crotch of the tree, from where
a rat snake had leapt in a breakout fast
and surged into mulch in its full vigour.

Swooping down on grasses, screaming aloud,
flitting in short flights, chased the angry flock,
the reptile right on its trail till too cowed,
it slithered to cover under a rock.

The babblers returned to the coral tree,
restless yet, and they checked for eggs, any
left in a mug of twigs, a nest on the tree,
fastened to a fork but found it empty.

Hurt, the babblers descended with a plaint
down to the ground, and slowly, the ruckus
tailed away and into their babbling, quaint,
the flock fell and flew for fruits to a ficus.

Peafowl on NH766

On highway seven-six-six, see a train.
It freights a whole load of blue eyes, spewing
blue smoke, on just two wheels slowly rolling,
changing tracks easily from black to green.

Now, on green tracks, a steep slope, it ascends.
It must be a hill train on a shorter route
to Mysore than this highway's winding route.
But who, so many eyes in a train, sends?

Now on a sharp curve, the train chugs away,
hooting a repeated warning trumpet
loud and harsh, a screaming heard as 'may-awe'.
There disappears, the eyes and the car last.

Now, on highway seven-six-six, see
rolling, without railroad cars, an engine.
It takes the same direction as the eye
wagon—for the eye train, a spare engine?

Common Kingfisher

Things in blue hue are ever eminent.
The sky, the sea, the peacock, distant hills,
cathedral windows, Van Gogh's Starry Night
and you are blue, kingfisher—no surprise.

Imagination, confidence, distance,
and harmony—things blue does represent—,
you embody fisher in abundance,
like the sky at the horizon, distant.

Are you the sky's dust, like a wheel, blue
spinning down on the trees, and while upon
the trees, how do you become a bird, blue
with skills beyond most birds' ideation?

No bird beats the confidence you exude
when you hold your wedge—the enormous bill—,
to shallow waters, and alert eyes—shrewd—,
at unsuspecting fishes on the shoal.

Then, when you select your swimming quarry,
how, with a bob of the head, do you assess
its distance from your bill's tip, on the sly,
and execute the final swoop, precise?

Clean and glassy, you want water always
in the ponds and streams, and if not, you exit
to where they are thus, and so I praise
your life in harmony with the planet.

Wise Owl Speaks

Cool is my short name, owl.
Foul, you call not, my scowl.
Style mine is sporting a cowl.
Prowl not by me; no howl!

Moot I, things, which I hoot.
Scoot, some men, at my toot.
Flute, I can't; I'm no coot.
Cute, my voice is not.

Brown is my formal gown.
Fawn, too, wears the same stain.
Down are brown birds on the lawn.
Frown not at things so plain.

Night, for me, is just right,
bright if moonlight is not.
Light, if low, I hate not;
flight of flies, there I sight.

Head big, mine can go round,
dread for rats on the ground.
Misread me not, my friend.
Need more, I hoot, indeed?

Being Cormorant

On a moored buoy that bobbed in backwater
bobbed a cormorant hanging its wet wings.
A boy with queries on several things
accosted it from a boat moored near.

Yes, the cormorant said, I shall answer
all your questions while, in this breeze, I hold
my wet wings like a cross; oh, grab ahold
of the rope lest you might fall in the water.

Unlike a duck, my wing feathers are not
water-repellent, so I endure
this cross after every fishing tour.
Otherwise, my wet wings would fly me not.

The lack of waterproofing is not
my deficiency—proficiency.
Once into the water, my feathers ply
to release air like a deflating duct.

I get density to drop me like a stone
to water's depths to even a sand-eel;
hooking it up, I up—that is my zeal.
But as a surface bird, the duck is known.

Yes, upping with wet wings is an issue.
There, I seek the help of the wind, and once
airborne, in rapid wingbeats pronto bounce
I from wetness, and strong is my tissue.

Yes, I have a habit of juggling fish
in the bill; look at me, boy, on this buoy.
I have a long neck, don't you see, my boy?
Spines not, head first, pass fish down it, I wish.

Sing not I, chirp not I, babble not I.
I shouldn't if I can't sing; I utter
just a deep croak, but it is no clutter.
Anyway, of fishing, I'll never be shy.

O boy, right now, I need to leave this buoy.
The cormorant soared on dry wings and low
over water in a straight line, well below
the boy's height, it flew on far off the boy.

Cormorant's Prayer

Ashore a lake so deep and vast
gracefully stood a little church,
facing waters extending much
to shores of pale blue, so distant.

Church's verdant headland had a cross
of blackish stone, one standing tall.
On it was Christ, a figurine still
in Passion, facing the waters.

Cormorants, a flock flying that way,
landed on the lake in a swooping dash.
Swimming, it hemmed a shoal of fish—
a silver lace slithering away.

The raft of blackish diving birds,
a hunting party charging on,
and beating waters dashing on,
drove the shoal to shallow waters.

The shoal saw itself brought to bay
and nothing further do it could.
Never win life's race, the hunted,
but do win the hunters, someway.

Past a stunning spell of fishing,
the hunters rose in flight on wings,
reaching fast on the crowns of trees,
started drying wings by sunning.

A lone bird idled by the shore,
detached from the flock atop trees.
It sat on a stake, motionless,
keeping its wings open wide.

Slender and open wings held still—
It was a cross on that black stake.
It sat as that cross on that stake
for a long time, alone and still.

When a fishing boat passed across,
rose that bird from its long musing
and sent a word to folk fishing.
'Do heed the cross and be a cross.'

'He gave me wings that make me fly,
bill with a hook that makes me fish,
feet with a web to swim to the fish.
As a black cross, I want to fly.'

Nilgiri Wood Pigeon

(Note: Nilgiri Wood Pigeon, endemic to the Western Ghats, is a large reddish-brown forest pigeon with a grey head and prominent black-and-white 'chessboard' on the hindneck. Its call is a langur-like 'who' followed by three or four quick-repeated deeper 'who; who; who.' Source: Salim Ali)

Sixteen stalwarts stood on each side, chessmen
on my board; I was once a champion,
sending challengers quickly to checkmate,
as a man in prelife, always au fait.

Sixty years and another sixteen: what
I had in my life-board human, and it
was life's checkmate, the way of all mortals,
and I, a soul, rose to heaven's portals.

Slowly then arrived, my time for new birth.
'A pigeon,' said God, 'on your rebirth,
with rusty-red wings, a wood pigeon,
and on your nape, a chessboard, champion,'

So down I flew as a pigeon with a
checkerboard on my nape; this is not a
cock-and-bull story but a chess-and-bird
account of what did occur on God's word.

Say, say, who? Who? Who? Who goes over there?
Awhile won't you kindly stay back, birder?
Won't you, with me, sit for a game of chess?
I have the board. Do you have the pieces?

White-breasted Waterhen

Sunless is today as if with night smudged.
Afield into my semi dark stroll, stray,
shaking stumpy chestnut tails, slaty grey
waterhen, slender and white-breasted.

The pair stealthily rises from the low swamp
to the lonely grassy path, foreseeing
no man out this noon as dark as gloaming.
The hens sense me, although I do not stomp.

Alarmed, they turn and hustle to the marsh
running one lap and winging another
and while on the wing, they are rather
inches off the ground to land on a bush.

From the bush, they leap to a web of reeds,
skulking deep in the dark tangle, but crack
soon to a hoarse grunt and then to a croak,
like an ode to darkness and cloudy skies.

The Dance of the Peacock

Blue-green wings open but swung sideways,
facing his harem of hens, a peacock
halts on a remote, lonesome jungle track
as dawning to a bright day slowly grows.

When in admiration stay, all the hens,
erects and fans, he, his ocellated
train, arched forward and slightly tilted
with a repeated quiver of the quills.

He minces as a Kathakali dancer
and prances from foot to foot. Struts,
he crabwise slowly in measured steps.
His joy is evident from his train's shiver.

As he jigs so, a gentle ruffling sound
rises from the jiggering of the eyes—
the freight of his loaded train that chugs.
With a flourish of his feet, he turns around.

Now, he displays his hindmost grey spokes
to the spectator hens, whose eyes have been
esteeming his colourful fan, blue-green,
and its stunning studs of pearlescent eyes.

Sparrows Attend Sunday Mass

'Cheer, cheer…' cheers gaily from the courtyard
of Vallarpadam's church, a house sparrow.
Black throat and chestnut back—it's a fellow.
Grey-brown, his pair, too, is about the yard.

In a flourish, he fluffs out plumes like a balloon
and takes a few steps as though on a skate.
Then, with rump arched up, wings drooped, and gait
arrogant, he struts along like a clown.

Now, the church bell rings, and the choir sing.
Apace soaring, the pair crosses the door
into the church and lands on a fissure
above the nave, in the old wooden ceiling.

In the name of Our Father, the mass begins.
The female sparrow sinks to quiet prayer,
   —like any devout—in the high shelter.
'Cheer, cheer, cheer,' devoutly the male hymns.

A Nestling of Wagtail

A baby bird peeped at the peep of dawn
beneath its mother's wings, inside tiny,
a home, a cup of a tuft of grasses drawn
on low a fork of a tree's trunk, huge, murky.

In a green and pristine riverine islet,
in a shingly river of a lively gush,
was that lone tree into waters, aslant
from little thickets lit in dawning's flush.

They were wagtails, a mama and her chick.
The chick was too hungry and so whiny,
and it lightly pecked at its mother's neck—
as if complaining, 'mammy, too hungry.'

Arose, the mammy from a dreamy sleep
up and down, wagging her tail—and noting,
way up was the sun, yet she was asleep.
She ran her bill on the fluff of her darling.

The nestling gaped its empty mouth, making
the mother glide out and soar on and on.
Across the river, she winged to outlying
shores to bring insects for her young one.

The baby bird was of an age that explores
and so, though hungry, it sought to waggle
its baby tail, which then rose in light jerks,
and then fell to shimmies—a whole wobble.

The birdie, wagging thus, dived onto
the forky footing of its shelter and, in
rapid short spurts, it propelled itself, ooh,
up and along the bulky trunk in fun.

An oarsman fishing that way threw his oar,
finding his way amid boulders and his
noisy rowing shocked the small explorer
upon the trunk, and it broke to a whiz.

Missing its grip, it fell from the tree and
that was the time a big eagle glid, though
the islet so low, which, in a swoop, lifted
the trophy of birdie, piercing it through.

At that time, the mother bird was in flight
over the stream with a beetle, staple
for her dear, whom in her nest she had left.
On she flew, on and on, with that beetle.

Seven Sisters

A flock, often of seven birds,
babbling on the woods' shady glade
every daybreak and eventide,
takes the cute name—seven sisters.

Sisters! What a name for a flock
of birds that shares every second
that it lives in its brief period
upon its world, the jungle dark.

Untidy, frowzy, and earthy brown,
jungle babblers band together
and that bond is their true power
to ward off raptors that swoop on.

Babblers' style is chatter constant
as they hop on, turning dry leaves,
and sometimes engage in disputes
that get settled in an instant.

Fussy, not are babblers—eating
anything on their way they find, like
a moth, a roach, a grain and the like
or fruits or nectar of trees blooming.

The centre is babblers of mixed
hunting parties of jungle birds
that wave uphill hunting insects—
an avian army united.

The winged bipeds' hunting party
admits several larger members:
drongoes, mynas, treepies—all, friends—
and they follow babbler birdie.

Bird is not the jungle babbler—
an idea; looks seldom matter;
deeds do. The jungle babbler,
the humble hopper, is a leader.

Sound of Solitude

Suddenly, from the hush of the wood,
as aloud a bird trills a note,
rid, I, my melancholy mood.
Suddenly, from the hush of the wood,
hark, I, the sound of solitude.
Soar, I, like a feather afloat
suddenly, from the hush of the wood,
as aloud a bird trills a note.

Junglefowl Cock

On a clearing green and grassy
popped a sickle—jet black, a tail.
As grasses parted, rustlingly,
emerged a cock of junglefowl.

A shining dawn sun came over
the grasses, hills and lantana.
Away strutting the grass cover,
the cute cock beaked a cicada.

Taut a neck and tail drooping,
shy and wary, always angry
and harsh, a warning grunt crowing
foraged along, the cock cutie.

Its bill was yellow, its iris dusky,
comb and the wattle crimson deep,
a neck with golden bars, waxy
and streaked a body grey, not deep.

A kite then approached, flying low
when to cover scuttled the cock
crowing awhile for fear of the foe
and then skulking, hushed in shock.

Malabar Parakeet

Bright, a glimmer came in a flash
far east in the blue hour sky.
Blue hills in sleep rose in a dash,
drawing a doodle in the sky.

The radiant sun on the hill's line
shattered its rays, drilling huge crowns
of trees asleep, reaching yard mine,
smiling at me, standing by a fence.

I heard a flight landing with a shrill,
atop a fig laden with fruits,
right in my yard, so woody still,
on roots acting impressive props.

Parakeets blue, swooping in haste,
hanging from fig, clutching at twigs,
reached beaks, red, at pendent fruits ripe,
swollen with pulp as red berries.

Bills cherry-red; fruits very red;
wings very blue; leaves very
green; boughs very grey—charmed
was I, by hues, very many.

A White-bellied Sea Eagle
Seeks a Casuarina Tree

A white aircraft with black-bordered wings
circles low by the seashore in India
on the western coast. Not landing, it flies
away over the seaboard. The media
won't report this air traffic incident
or this pilotless flight's misery.
For a safer landing elsewhere, the craft
that soars in the cloudless skies, wintery,
is a sea eagle back from a fishing flight
and finding its dear casuarina tree
being felled. A deep bowl of dry sticks that
was the raptor's humble treetop aerie
now lies badly under a downed limb, crushed
on the beach sands. The casuarina—the last
one on this beach—now falls when obscured,
the sea eagle melts in the clouds, distant.

No more would listen, the local fishers,
to the eagle's honk, nor would they see
it, lifting sea snakes on its talons.
O, approaching fishing boat, inform me—
Have you seen airborne, a sea eagle
seeking a casuarina for an aerie?
and maybe, by now, flying on its tail
in pain, its partner, with a honk goosy?

Lament of the Greater Adjutant Stork

(Note: Greater Adjutant-Stork is generally silent away from the nest, where the bird utters loud grunting, croaking, mooing and roaring sounds and indulges in bill-clattering displays typical of most storks. In the nineteenth century, it was abundant in Calcutta and Burma. The bird is now on the verge of extinction, with only eight hundred to twelve hundred mature individuals. Causes of decline include the destruction of potential nesting, feeding and roosting sites and probably poisoning by pesticides. Source: birdsoftheworld.org)

Like an irked pig, grunt, I.
Like a lone frog, croak, I.
Like a sad cow, moo, I.
Like a sore cat, roar, I.

These are tongues mine many
though you hear me these days
as a rather steady
rattling of mandibles.

When one's clan perishes,
one loses all the words.
Know this: my bill rattles
my prayer to the gods.

Gods, keep my clan extant!
Sapiens, heed men extinct—
the great hominids, past.
Who wants that sad fate?

Once, a General taught
me the footstep, my gait,
a measured martial foot—
thus, I get called Adjutant.

Calcutta was our base
where we enjoyed space
and edibles plenty once
and trees in abundance.

But from there, chased out like
refugees, we are stuck
mainly in Assam; luck
is nowhere by our side.

Grant, in Bihar, too, hide,
some of us opposed
for dropping from the roosts,
grub in smelly crumbs.

Forget not—we scavenge
for you; you keep a grudge,
although for moorage,
all day, we scavenge.

Can't we, man, bird and beast,

live in accord? Extinct,
no species should be left.
Of hope, make not me bereft.

Silence of the Frogmouth

A varied smell had the forest:
of elephants tearing twigs yonder,
of blooms from many a thicket,
of earth soggy of night's downpour.

I heard a varied sound deep in:
on treetops of waiting raptors,
on the grass of peacocks' trains, in
the damp peat of vocal croakers.

I reached a stand of thin, low trees,
and a pair of frogmouths silent,
small birds, cryptic and mysterious,
their feathers like dry leaves finest.

Under twigs sat the pair huddled,
leaning against each other's bodies,
sleepy, still, and looking muddled,
with wedgy beak and mouth froggy.

That was a rare sighting inland,
of a fragmented population,
afar, overseas, an island
being its home, lost in isolation.

The silence sank in by the pair,
distant from the birds of the day,
was of fear of foreseen danger,
lurking close by and not away.

Was of all creatures, that silence,
of men and beasts and all the birds:
the helplessness of all in exile;
the fear and pain of refugees.

A Chat with a Taiga Flycatcher

April 2022

On the crown of a pine tree trills a bird,
like the creak of a branch in passing wind.
To a short looping sally, down it swoops
on a dragonfly in quick beats of wings.

The bright orange patch with a wash of red,
right on the throat of the teeny grey bird,
swipes me to the surprise of a very rare
sighting—Are you a Taiga Flycatcher?

My, my! You said my name, my dear birder.
Aye, I'm from the Taiga woods, birdwatcher,
of pine, larch, and spruce of Siberia,
boreal woods of conifers in Russia.

When you are home in the Taiga, you wear,
I know, a necktie, brighter and redder
for your merry breeding season; tell me,
how is Munnar, verdant gardens of tea?

I had a winter well-spent in these lands.
To your hills and lea, I pay my regards.
Morrow, I shall leave for my Taiga home,

being well into April's return time.

I'm so sad that you are leaving so soon.
Home is home, I know, and before monsoon,
for the long flight, you must sure be airborne.
In rough winds, you should not be left forlorn.

I need to cross India to Pak, and then
Afghan to Ural Mountain range when
I'll be towards northwest Siberia.
Ahead, I shall be home in the Taiga.

Buddy, be wary when by the Urals.
At war is Russia with Ukraine; the skies
of Western Russia about the Urals
maybe risky, and you weigh just ten grams.

War? Again? I faced crises in Afghan
several times, and you say, now Ukraine
fronts a fight; I had flown in through calm skies.
How will I fly home across the war skies?

WOODS

Tonight in the Dark Woods

The night in the woods under a starry sky
is what I see right now; dark is tonight
the woods, sans the glow of fireflies that fly,
and the moon, a faint crescent indistinct.

When polluted not is the dark night-time,
burning candles, millions are shining
stars on the galactic disc all the time,
as now they are up in the skies glowing.

Cloudy not is this October night's sky.
The woods, in a field of black surreal
mellowed out in a whiff of starlight, lie,
abound with trees in a phantom profile.

I have visitors here whose dark contours
I can trace around pinpricks in the glow:
A boar, a gaur, a herd of deer yonder.
I hear bushes break as the pinpricks flow.

Again, I hear the woods—a sailing glide
and a flap of wings and then a loud call,
a harsh note repeated in a quick slide
like grinding rice in a quern, a stone mill.

The one who grinds rice well into the night
I think I know: nightjar. On moonlit nights,
its call is louder, yet now, in starlight
amidst metallic calls, hawks it, insects.

I want to scale a tall rock to lie face up
scanning the skies, and dripping to sleep,
dreaming of tigers for prey in the lookup
tonight, in the dark woods as the stars peep.

Wind in the Woods

Under a silver oak sat I
in the woods, listening to the wind
flirting with oak tree leaves and
telling them bye with a deep sigh.

Sank, the meadow lodged for a while,
pounded by the wind with a whiz.
Back from goose flesh, with a fizz,
the tract of grass sprang up in style.

I saw the wind smite a mango.
The tree's sprays bobbed, agreeing
to what the wind whispered, passing
in haste beside a stream to disco.

To the wind's loud, sibilant flute,
the underbrush of bamboo danced
and danced gaily from the streamside
with a loud hiss and a long hoot.

Stands of trees stayed for the halloo
of the wind, and so it had to hurry
along but though in a flurry,
to the scrub, it had an aah and ooh.

Shades of Green in the Woods

Between cyan and yellow abides green,
and in so many shades in verdant woods,
of which the deepest is chlorophyll green,
the intense green for photosynthesis.

The purple-green of tender mango leaves
evolves through very many hues, green,
until it grows to deep green, and so does
the mango fruit to yellow through greens.

The jack tree has a gradient of green
from the peak of the crown to the foliage
of lower branches—the darkest in sheen,
which the barbet uses for camouflage.

Grey-green are the papery leaves of teak.
Palms in the wind wave flags of intense green.
Groves of bamboo dance in green cloths, sleek.
Grasses display countless arrays of green.

Green frog, vine snake, parrot, leafbird, tiny
grasshoppers, and so on goes the checklist
of creatures green in the deep woods, shady,
that stay disguised in the wood's life greenest.

Forest Fire

A dash of hiss and fizz was the wildfire
across the grasses, with a tail of wind.
The grasses in yellow—their summer wear—
fell in the fire, falling dead, blade by blade.

Like on wings, dragons black, coiled up, smoke
from the outcrop—no longer grassland but
immersed in flakes of ash, a land soot-black—
bereft of any life. From there, a jet
was the fire as ember on wind's wings, wild,
to the trees yonder standing gagged in the hills
in smoke. The alliance of fire and wind
saw its way to the tall trees—first, like frills
yellow, and then like licking tongues, and then
like amber serpents thousands—eating them
and then, like a volcano eruption
blasting high up, pronto crumbling them.

With booms and bangs bounded along the trees,
the crown fire lighting the hills in deep yellow.
Of soot, the sky went jet as burning trees
like tall chimneys spewed smoke with a bellow.
Hills had charred snakes in many a cranny.
The soot, in part, was bees before the fire
and birds and mammals which failed to flee.
Advanced to new flanks, still hungry, the fire.

Into the Woods

Into the woods, like into a temple, I entered.
Sung as a duet, a hymn by wind and brook.

Found I, God, in every blade of grass that danced
and every leaf that waved from many a trunk.
The silence was the long prayer my lips whispered
as I padded the carpet of thick humus dank
on my way into the mystery of woods, awed,
through cicada's litanies from brook's bushy bank.

My heart leapt in delight, of all shackles relieved.
I fell into a déjà vu: my home; I'm home back.
Of all the wounds the world inflicted on me healed,
I wandered deep into the woods, as free as a lark,
thinking about pantheism. I found my God,
joy, hope, and happiness in the woods, dark.

Into the woods, like into a temple, I entered.
Sung as a duet, a hymn by wind and brook.

Commensalism

It's my everyday sight in the swamp
when I walk by it in the dawn, cattle
egrets on stick-like black legs settle
on herds of grazing buffaloes that stomp
in the thick muck and lift skilfully,
hiding bugs from the bovid's fluff fuzzy
and beak them; often, they go for a hop
down onto the lush grass to the little
insects, flushed by the tread of the cattle.
The bovid esteems egrets' partnership
and the bumpy hitch-hike and gentle
stalking of flies even off its tactile
eyelids, bereft of harm and hardship.

One day, I saw two crows down on a swoop
to a buffalo's head when from its tail,
an egret was picking sheep ked; heckle
did not, egret, but croaked, 'Well, crows, go stoop
on flies, but hurt in no way, my big pal.'
'Oh, no,' cawed the crows, 'we shall be mindful.'
'Devour as much as you want, crows; the swamp
has ample flies for all birds, and the cattle
flush them out to us; birds never quarrel
here for insects,' egret hissed from the rump.

Jungle Safari

The safari huffed along jungle tracks
like a motorised beast with a long tail
of smoke that often wound around branches
of trees holding variegated crowns, tall.

Red trails scarring the surreal green
of the woods—damp of night's rains—were lonely,
but for jaywalking peacocks out in the dawn,
jerkingly dragging their trains rustlingly.

From the van's winding course, narrow footpaths
diverged to untold depths of the jungle,
like the nervures in a moth's wing; grasses
lazily sagged on them like a green frill.

The wheeler infringed on the great silence
of the woods, which even the wind honoured
by not howling but just showing fondness
to trees in just a mellow whisper hushed.

A flock of green bee-eaters sank upon
a stand of bamboo dissolving in its
lanceolate leafage, and thus hidden,
it, too, fell in the stillness of the woods.

Ahead, a proud herd of deer turned its heads.
While a robust stag—the herd's leader—
walked along, the hinds halted, their eyes
scanning the mascara of female riders.

An antediluvian patriarch
with a shabby black coat—an elephant—
outreached a tree's leafy limb, a vast arch
was its trunk as it tore off an offshoot.

A tribe of langurs fancied not aliens
wheeling; restless, it boohooed, ascending
to dense crowns in quick and excited leaps
making lofty trees panic, shivering.

Wended the way, dipping in shallow creeks
and mounting hardly rugged outcrop often
the safari, dust on wings as a wake
after it as birds sang to the sun in fun.

Bamboo and Wind

A stand of bamboo—wherever it stands,
very often in quiet marginal lands—
has humble looks yet imposing stature.
It's a joy to see it—a gift of nature.

A lively lover, wind, keeps a regular
tryst with bamboo, gently stroking her,
and she giggles every time in answer,
whirling pronto like a bonny dancer.

A flock of sparrows is a viewer, frequent,
to the bamboo's jig and hop in delight
as her suitor fingers her like a fiddle.
Then, delighted, the flock breaks to a trill.

Beside lonely brooks, bends bamboo towards
the water, when in a hug winds her, the wind.
And she, in the bourn, beats herself—her way
of venting her dislike, 'Naughty! Away!'

On windless days, wildly moody, are woods
when branches stay silent and still on trees.
And for bamboo, it is but bugaboo,
as it saddens her—the wind saying boo.

Silence of the Woods

Of things winsome, fancy I of deep woods,
I speak foremost of its silence, endless,
but for leaves' notes as they flop down lifeless,
and from stands of trees, random calls of birds.

The jungle is a temple of prayers quiet.
One admits it when its hush is sometimes
breached by a wind soughing over the trees,
and when tribes of langurs shrill a lament.

The distant jungle brooks babble feebly—
a cradle song, delicate and mellow.
In alarm herds of does do call, shallow,
though their bells are, as they dart off swiftly.

At times, cicadas flout the woods' silence;
the frog, too, joins them but heeding intense
the tranquil of woods, go they remorseful,
eyes shut at times, quiet and regretful.

When I wander in the world's din, hapless,
I wish I would vanish deep in still woods.
Of things winsome, fancy I of deep woods,
I speak foremost of its silence, endless.

Dawn in the Western Ghats

Atop the hills, the sun is a lamp red.
Awakes, in haste, the sleeping night, alarmed.
Twilight flees through trees, of the sun afraid.
Dawn, it's dawn in the woods, very vivid.

Wakened, drongos sing to the sun an ode.
A wind is with music in the background.
Alight, mynas on boughs chirping aloud.
Dawn, it's dawn in the woods, very vivid.

Mist is afloat, and the vale very dimmed.
A thrush carols sweetly from the brushwood.
The flicker of lamps from hill homes drops dead.
Dawn, it's dawn in the woods, very vivid.

On its beat is junglefowl in a parade.
The cock is in vigil, leading his squad.
Clucking lowly, the hens strut just behind.
Dawn, it's dawn in the woods, very vivid.

On the ascent to the skies overhead,
the red sun whitens and cracks to beams crude,
spewing a stunning sheen on the hillside.
Dawn, it's dawn in the woods, very vivid.

Yonder Hills

Yonder hills, from far down as I watch you,
a brim with wonder are my seeking eyes.
What is under that unclear, eerie blue
that you wear but with unkempt wrinkles?

What is that you conceal at this instant?
What ilk of flocks of showy wings are on
to fruit-laden branches with a sweet note
alongside your wooded shoulders airborne?

Are there herds on your verdant grasslands
upward from grazing throwing head, wary
of lurking hazards and shifting shadows
in parting grasses of big cats, scary?

How do you, I wonder, gather water
for that steep silvery descent that, like
a glazy white garland dangles down your
blue-draped neck as a jewel, dreamlike.

To your solace and eternal stillness,
pronto, I want to wind my wild ways.
I die; I die for your plunging silence
and endless quietness myself, yonder hills.

A Night Safari at Nelliyampathy

Nightlife is not in a club or a bar
where day life spills into the night
with the misnomer nightlife; to daylight,
the owl is an uncertain caller—
We don't note it as the owl's day life.
Little this thought takes on me as my night
safari rolls from a jungle resort
to a moonless night and nightly wildlife
alongside a tea garden. Fireflies like
garlands aglow adorn afar, oak crowns.
With silvery trunks lifting pruned crowns—
like hairy heads—shady oaks are ghostlike.

Staked down to the hills by oaks is the vast
spread of tea with ruffles several.
Hiding in it, somewhere deep, goes vocal
a brood of buzzing cicadas which, past
a crescendo dips to a sudden hush.
The patch yonder is with pinpricks aglow—
a herd of deer transfixed by the beam low
of the engine halting beside the brush.
Two blackish boulders bounce via the tea.
'Elephants,' whispers the man at the wheel.
The matriarchs gradually amble
away across the macadam to a tree.

Now is the turn of a hefty bison,
standing still in the tea like an outcrop
hooking the riders in a stare down deep,
before turning as though with an, 'I won.'
Hearing hooting owls rolls on the wheeler
slowly through the marvels of the nightlife—
apparitions with eyes aglow—of wildlife.
Nightlife is not in a club or a bar.

Forest Bathing

The grass goes lodged as on and on I stroll.
A whiff I catch of green leaf volatile—
conveys grass, 'Man, wander but hurt me not.'
The tranquil jungle trail, like a serpent,
slithers into grass, scrub, and wetland.
See that tree yon, in shades myriad crowned.
Fails me, its name, but what a delight it
does give and how much birds do like that roost.

Prick me not, o thorn, pull me not, o thorn.
I'm your guest, o thorn, out from dull my screen
and way from tiresome work; blessed are you
to own a home so primal, where doves coo.
O, here, I hear a giggle—a stream distant
in lush stands somewhere of trees verdant.
A harp is always coursing water.
Is not a melody, monsoon rains pour?

Takes off there, a bird blue, from a bough bald.
Lift me, God, turning me alar—a bird,
over ancient trees to soar, so from skies
I eye this sea, this bliss in all its hues.

A Trek to a Montane Grassland

That was a rocky trail with mossy scars,
adrip with seep—the sweat of weary rock.
It was a tough hike up the mountain's flank.
Far down, died out, the bark of village dogs.

My taut legs conked out but with a warm smile,
the peak, and with cheers, the breeze ushered me,
alone scaling the mountain still with glee.
Soloed through dawn, I, with no more boggle.

I reached the peak's goatee, verdant a stand
of tall magnolia trees, jumping a cliff,
so waned, tapered, as it sank in the glyph.
Ahead, I saw my goal: the vast grassland.

A swirl of grasses fell in dance over
my path shortly, dragging me, when like oars
my hands rolled in a sea of tall grasses,
whose rapid eddies rapped me all over.

Thus, wading lemongrass—that with sharp awn
gored my skin, yelling in my ears—I slunk,
not surefooted, but in whirls like a drunk,
as wind wafted, a whiff of tart lemon.

In came a challenge—a giant, black rock
with a dark maw—from grasses like a huge
hippo with jaws agape and looking rogue,
but I did find in it a pass, a dike.

Tilting within that tight, hazy cavern
at last, arrived I at the lip of a bluff
that dangled from a sky of frothy fluff
and far below, saw I, farmlands, unknown.

Atop the final rock where the peak fell,
lay I, supine under the sky, as flicks
of mist drifted past me up from gorges,
and wind circled the grasses with a howl.

ANIMALS

Tiger Cool

Daddy, daddy cool, daddy, daddy cool.
Tiger, tiger cool, tiger, tiger cool.
Tiger takes me coolly to Boney M.
Calm is ever the tiger, the gem
of the forest, on jungle tracks so quiet
except when it is in a hunting sprint.
Scratch at a tree; stop for a drink, a drink;
stare at the striped reflection in the brook;
peer in wonder all around from the brush;
sleep away free time; shun undue ambush—
Daddy has this to-do list to stay cool.
Tiger, tiger cool, tiger, tiger cool.

Lion-tailed Macaque

1
Silent Valley, The Western Ghats, 1995

Memories of the verse 'Ode to the Tree',
the primaeval forest, silent, evoked
and the seventies' 'Save Silent Valley
Move' as I on her rich humus floor walked.
Under the green awning of trees, sprawling—
lofty, splendid, ancient, evergreen—
wan was the dawning with a wind wailing
across a valley, pristine in green sheen.

The crown of a fig had a short jitter.
A couple of monkeys ran up its boughs
after throwing me a quick scowl, bitter
and pronto swung away along the limbs.
A tuft of hair tipped their prehensile tails,
and they had silver manes—lions by manes
and tails, but monkeys about trunk and limbs.
To be away from the man were their pains.

2
Valparai, The Western Ghats, 2015

Forty hairpins uphill the Monkey Falls,

plateaued Valparai as I drove my car
along a hill road, sandwiched by live walls
of trees bordering plantations that scar
the woods with patches of coffee and tea.
Under the shades of canopy pruned thin,
ran, I, eyes on fields of coffee and tea
for birdlife out on a sunny day's dawn.

Then, on an old sloping roof, I noticed
a black monkey and pulled up the engine.
Down the roof's clay tiles, the primate gild.
And soon, I saw it on the car's side screen
clinging, from where it vaulted to the front
windscreen—its jaws agape, and its canine
teeth revealed like sharp wedges, betel stained.
It flicked its lion tail and jerked its silver mane.

Spoke it, no word, but read I, its red eyes—
Where is my intact canopy, my fruits?
Why did you fragment my clan, sapiens?
I need my food so, give me your biscuits.

Malabar Giant Squirrel of Sim's Park

Vast lawns, bloom beds and crude rockeries
in contours natural of a wooded dale
rich in bushes and flowery creepers
make the sprawling Sim's Park a dreamlike vale.

On thick mats of roots, many a tree fern,
prodigious Queensland kauri, sacred
Rudraksha—whose berries, blue bear beads, brown
for prayer lei in Hinduism—revered,
coniferous pines, magnolias holding
blossoms like white bowls, calling to the mind
myths, tall Phoenix palms, and thus the listing
goes of trees with which the garden is lined.

The dawn chorus was still alive and on
camellia blossom finches were in a flit
when alone, I hiked an elevation
of Sim's after Scimitar babblers' flute.
The winding way wound up at a scrub, where
sagged a rufous tail like a bottlebrush
from a tree. Showing me a short, stern stare,
a giant squirrel rushed in a flush.

Shaking twigs wildly, rapidly leapt
on the canopy like a bird, red-brown,

the squirrel from tree to tree and past
tall pines, on a ficus, it settled down.
Up and down the berry-bearing branches,
on an appraising trip, it cherry-picked
cherry-red a berry. Holding its arms
in prayer, it feasted on that fruit, red.

A Baby Monkey's Tour to the Town

A baby monkey scaled a town-bound truck,
for he had no fun in the hill's woods, dark.
When the truck halted by the town's big park,
the baby found it good to disembark.
Of fruits on a huge mango tree, awe-stuck,
he climbed through a mango branch, very thick.

Munching mangoes, the baby watched the fun
romping kids had upon a sprawling lawn.
Excited thus, he swung up and down the crown
of the mango tree howling in joy when
he saw a trough of twigs that had blue-green
eggs—a clutch of four, banded with brown.

The baby knew nothing of eggs but saw
balls, which, down upon the lawn, children threw
at each other. For the heck of a throw,
he seized from the clutch an egg and threw
it down. The egg broke and bled yellow.
Beaming, the baby gave his nose a blow.

A house crow, feasting on a dead sewer
rat digging deep its bill by brush yonder,
left the rat and flew to the egg-lifter,
cawing loud and past a quick hop over

its nest, it dived on the baby visitor.
To the crow's caw winged in crows, a murder.

The kids in the park soon saw a weird chase
of a baby monkey by many crows.
The baby ran and ran and ran. The crows
bullied him and bullied him all his ways
till he flew to a passing truck with goods
loaded and rolled off, dreaming of the woods.

A Trunkful of Love

In her trunk, she brought a trunkful
of water from the stream, the mother
elephant; her calf, like a boulder,
lay there, amidst the bushes, still.

Emptied, she, her full trunk upon
the head of her baby son
and did quickly stir him with one
foot, not yet knowing he was gone.

Petted and patted him, her trunk.
Then, did kneel she, beside him with
what he would surely like, the pith
of plantain, but still was his trunk.

At last, she strode around her son
realising what it all meant.
From her, a trumpet—a lament—
flew out—My son! My son! My son!

Before the Bench

1

I am a farmer in the hills,
growing on my farm many corms.

Abuts a dense forest, my field,
and so, I've visitors—beasts, crude.

They do lift from my rich soil
part of what I raise by toil.

A dirty boar sporting two tusks
snorts its way during silent nights.

Digs it, the earth like a dozer,
pulling out my ripe crops, tuber.

After a feast of tasty yams,
dozes off, not it—dozes fields.

Never have I invited the boar
but it gatecrashes for dinner.

I pray, call the boar vermin.
I can then meet it with a gun.

2

I am a boar; I have a tale.
Lend me an ear if you have time.

I have two tusks that are so keen.
I plough with tusks fields in the rain.

I want you, man, to know my work.
I'm helping you with your farm task.

But know this: you pay no wages.
So, I nibble some of your corms.

It seems you want me not to work.
If so, give me my forests back.

You've taken my land for your field.
I lost my tasty rhizomes wild.

Now you want to call me vermin.
You want to kill me with a gun.

Have you read Orwell's ancient tale?
I imply his plot, not his tail!

But believe not I, in revolt.
Yet, boundaries one must respect.

I shall never make the first move.

You trigger conflicts that you love.

Give me my forest—my garden.
No, neither of us is vermin.

Buffalo and Egret

'After a mud bath, I'll go for
grazing,' said the bovid,
a water buffalo sinking
in mud, but for its head.

'Never have I beheld like this
a swamp as big with grass
and mud, and egret flies for you.
What a splendid landmass.'

An egret perched upon a bush
and eager not to coat
a splash of slush on its feathers,
whistled a happy note.

The bovid rolled its frame in mud.
'Lo! The earth,' it lowed low,
'hugs me and hums her ancient tune,
always when I wallow.'

'Listen to it; come with me for
a ride.' Rose the bovid.
The egret winged to the bovid's back,
and its perch hitched forward.

Flip-flop, flip-flop, flip-flop, flip-flop—
in jerks marched the buffalo.
The rider rode, eyes on the mire,
and ears at earth's hum low.

Where a Cow is More Than a Cow

Going by years thus far,
younger than the farmer,
but going by lifespan,
older than the farmer,
was she, the old cow brown.

A calf was she, a heifer,
when the farmer bought her
and walked her to his home
from the barn of a dealer
and put her on his farm.

For two full days, she mooed
in her little new shed,
having moved from her mum
to live ever parted,
and so, losing her calm.

But kind was the farmer
and he, with love, rose her,
giving the name Browny,
for brown was her colour.
Alone, there stayed Browny.

In time, a dam she became,

and her calf had the same
colour as her, a pet
of the farmer who came
every hour to pet it.

When the young calf went weaned,
farmer sold it, cash-strapped,
and this went on, Browny
calving and calf when weaned
sold out soon for money.

Then, with age, no longer
Browny suckled, and her
calving ended. No more
milch, she was. The farmer,
yet, kept her as before.

The farmer knew of old age.
He, too, was of that stage.
And, so, he liked Browny
to stay right there for life—
milch or not milch, Browny.

Browny was yet of use
since for the farm, she gave
dung, that the crops in that
farm of many a legume—
farmer's sole income—ate.

As time flew by, too old
grew the farmer to tend
his Browny, so one day,

he let her from the shed
go, but she kept her stay.

The farmer was alone
as there he had no kin,
sans his Browny, his friend,
who mooed her affection
all these years from her shed.

But that day, too, arrived
which the farmer feared.
Helpless, he found no way
to someway avoid
selling Browny away.

He was short of money,
and he was too puny
even to reach the barn.
He knew the place Browny
would walk to, with no scorn.

Browny walked from the shed
beside a stranger, shoved.
She paused by her master,
whose tears, as she looked,
fell on her creased brown fur.

With a moo, she set out
on her last walk and at
the waving blades of green
grass wayside, she looked not,
droved on and on and on.

Spider and Cicada

On a bush sat a cicada,
welcoming dusk. A drone
was its ode—although a bit odd—
to the night—like a groan.

'Good,' said a giant wood spider,
'If anything is a song,
it is your cadence, cicada.
You are pretty a gong.'

A bong—what the giant spider
heard in reply. Candid
it was, 'Good words, buddy, spider.'
'Night!' farewell spider bid.

A friendship began on a chirp.
One day, the spider said,
'Cada, your wings are wonderful—
fine films of tender thread.'

'I love to pitch something with that
stuff, an orb and a stage.
I shall host there, my fly friends,
when a show you may stage.'

'Why not? Why? I shall sing a song
that should humble the lark,
and that would leave only the frog
to match me in this park.'

The spider spun an immense web
that had great needlework
akin to the cicada's wings,
and it was great artwork.

Then came the day of the party.
One by one, the visitor
flies vanished, and at last, the host
ate the song and the singer.

Bears of Daroji

A ridge of tor is Daroji,
a mesa abrupt on the sides,
adorned with scanty scrub jungles—
home of sloth bears, bulky.

The sun shows no mercy to it,
heating it like a red-hot pan,
when the day reaches noon,
until eventide of soft light.

Its trees look very stunted,
Shrubs, a tangle of prickly thorns—
snarled, messy, browny masses—
on a gneiss bed, vast and jagged.

Its hardy plateaued crest surmounts
stony vales of plant life, thirsty,
dreaming of rain that is scanty
in vast a land of towering tors.

It sports hush—uneasy—in hot
noon, breached at times by peacocks
in screams of rage, dashing across
heatwave floating upon the butte.

Come the evening, the sun relents,

the hill cools off, the black rocks
shadow and the wearied trees
sigh a gentle breeze on their crowns.

Then, from the dark caves in a shroud
of massive, rounded rocks arise
phantoms like black rocks busted loose,
and they tumble down the stone bed.

The ghostly figures shortly take
their bodily form: shaggy fur;
a bulbous snout; a long lower
lip; around the face, a mane thick.

No rolling stones—a sleuth of bears
dropping through its rocky country—
on its way to the low valley
seeking great a meal of termites.

To a blazing pyre, the sun dips
on the western sky—its turn
to get burnt up shortly therein
and lost as ashes in darkness.

Then, when gloaming palls, the rocky
peak and peacocks roost upon trees,
bears gore downhill's anthills,
with their claws like sickles, spiky.

A day dies on the rocky land
and the dark scrub woods hear the suck
of black beasts slurping ants, snouts stuck
on mounds of red earth, pretty hard.

Rabid

I saw, on a shack's stoop, a quiet dog
eyeing morning walkers and, with a ball,
boys. The dog wagged its love when on a slog
I passed it. 'No dog, our ball, not your doll,'
bawled a boy when the dog showed interest
in the ball that cruised to it. 'Rabid dog,'
yelled a scamp, and he pelted the first
stone that, to a quick dart, propelled the dog.

The gang went berserk after the canid,
armed with stones and sticks, dumping their ball.
Excited, some youthful walkers joined
the chase, shouting. 'Rabid dog; see, in loll
is its tongue,' one expert pantingly said.
The dog—steady on its hotfoot—outran
its chasers and, into a thicket, ploughed.
From that safe cover, it barked, 'Rabid men!'

A Meditating Water Buffalo

Parched is this swampland in hostile, hot May.
Here, every dawn, I see waterhens
which on my footfall, skulk sank in grasses;
cattle egrets, upon their plumage, grey,
adorn a wash of beige for breeding;
with a gait—prudent, proud—purple moorhens,
deftly stalking fen frogs; calm pond herons;
reprising from treetop a chattering
melody, the white-breasted kingfisher.
Making my dawns, dawns, joining the bipeds
in equal dimensions from quadrupeds
is a buffalo that, for its master,
lifts its head often from its inert rest
in the silt. I feel it takes my footfall
for the ploughman, who, in the interval
of some hours, pops up to check on his best
buddy black. Today, after a wet night
of summer rain, passing by the marshland,
behold, I, the buffalo, in a pond
not deep that it has dug in rain-soaked silt.
Its little pond, where its body went, sank,
sans head has brown banks built of mud,
where some eight egrets in alert guard stand.
The buffalo has its eyes shut, face blank.
I know; it is in meditation, deep.

What is it that it quietly ponders—
a long silent prayer for more showers,
a devotion for early monsoon sweep?

Jasmine and Moth

Utters a hoot, an owlet, from a bough.
To a glow sallow rises the new moon.
A young twining vine of jasmine, now
to a smile, unlocks cute white lips, and soon
goes infused the dooryard—dim, desolate—
with a sweet aroma that awakens
from deep prayer an ochre moth dormant.
In the night, quiet, he sees the parting lips.

And senses he, a tempting scent. Rises
he, on wings from what now he sees as dull
a way to waste a night in devotions.
The night is not a time to heed the soul.
Drawn to the shy smile of the jasmine spray,
the moth wings his way to steal a soft kiss.
Then to the next tempting smile, he does sway,
then to the next, and next, and next in bliss.

Hermit Crab

Does to death a left shell or skull allude?
To life, it does, I say. A mollusc dead
left a shell, which is my den—I headed
inside to be ever a hermit, prude.

Thus encased, the beating of waves, I brave.
Lacking my own hard shell, I'm a crossover—
a crab's body with a mollusc cover.
Reuse, recycle —I say from my cave.

A hermit, I pray from my shell shelter
for the mollusc that left its bony shell
for me to use, so by the sea, I dwell.
Who am I—back in life, that dead donor?

Reuse, recycle—I say from my cave.

PLANTS

The Wail of a Tree

'Timber,' screams out the lumberjack.
The tree, dismembered of its limbs
and roots, to bole, shivers as the jack
rapidly heads to a safe distance.

Aslant to the flank of its deep wounds
the bole breaks, by its weight, its pith
and the oldest growth ring that holds
it for a wink more to the earth.

With a wail, tumbles the tree, grand,
and pounds the ground in thunder,
and it does bounce once but drops dead.
'Hooray,' hollers the woodcutter.

The taproot deep inside the earth,
unaware still of the tree's collapse,
continues sucking from the depth
water that it sends up sans lapse.

The stump bleeds wherever the axe
battered it, silently bearing pain.
It had fought the logger's keen axe
that tore its flesh, although in vain.

As it feels water from the root,
the gutsy stump ceases, stoical.
It does break down in pain, acute.
Tearful, stands still, it, so soulful.

Indian Coral Tree

The coral of the rainforest,
coral tree is a friend of the farmer—
It gives shade to his estate;
it supports his vines of pepper.

Is its grey spiky ramose trunk
vitality in metaphor?
Its blossom decks many a park
in scarlet by the late winter.

Its bloom is the chicken's wattle.
Its thorn is the tiger's sharp claw.
Its leaf is a fodder model.
Its pod is food but not as raw.

When it is in bloom in winter,
coral is a tree, wearing fire.
Are blooms on thorny stalks sweeter,
and is it why thorns roses bear?

Adorn thorns, the stalks of life's hard
years, which, as Shelley wails, do bleed
the man but rosy times of win ford
the streams of later years, indeed.

Under a coral tree in bloom,
as I pen this, I see starlings
sip nectar from its scarlet blossom—
a happy flock of woods' darlings.

Memories of the Paddy Field

I want to slog across the bunds
of damp fields of juvenile rice,
wading in slush and watching toads
skitter under the grass in a trice.

I want to see in the paddies, the hop
of young rice girls in parrot greens
to the fabulous music of a troupe—
wind, water, and an army of frogs.

I want to see a water snake,
from flooded paddies, stalk a frog
in a quick leap off the slough and rake
the shoots of rice in the peat bog.

I want to see egrets, a flock—
across the rice flats, with yellow
bills—stick around and halt to hawk
fishes in sweeps, not so mellow.

I want to smell a paddy flat.
My boyhood, I would then smell—
the smell of rice plants, mucky peat,
bog and frog, and ploughing bull.

Golden Shower Tree

Golden blooms on a thousand pendulous
racemes, silver trunk, scanty pinnate leaves—
This tree is stunning in this spring of bliss.

Fond of gold is this beauty, sporting gems
all over her head and as go sheenless
old gold, purges them from tress, this lass.

Indeed, a princess is she—see, she stands
on a golden carpet, and her crown shines—
in the spring sun—of myriad prized gems.

The Black Rose of Ooty's Rose Garden

The slopes of Elk Hill hold hopes as roses.
Adorn these flowers, Ooty's very heart.
Even when anguished, stroll into roses,
and go exuding delight from the heart.

Under living tunnels, where ramblers hold
white blossoms slim, reflect on purity
and probity—virtues which always mould
life's meaning even in obscurity.

Floribunda and hybrid tea roses
in myriad shades, wave not just flowers—
from the terraces, they are upon, wishes
too for peace in life and happier times.

Look at each colour that the roses wear
and link it to moments in your journey
brief in this world, like red for love and care
and pink for thankfulness and ample joy,

Take orange for the zeal that does walk
one a long way; link rapport with yellow.
Thus, revisit your life past as you look
at roses in this park on your walk, slow.

And before you go, look at me, walker—
a black rose to hold no colour routine.
No hope, adieu—is that black, walker,
the dye of death or a sad cessation?

Black fully absorbs light that falls on it.
Is happiness white, and is sadness black?
How can black be sad if it absorbs light?
Rosy is not, still is a rose, a rose, black.

Touch-Me-Not Plant

'I touch it, and it folds its leaves,'
wonders a girl child, 'It's so shy.'
She whirls along to all the plants
that wear the same globose, rosy
flower heads and runs her fingers
gently on their leafage to sigh,
when blushfully go the leaves
folded. Says she, 'So shy, so shy.'
Her mum from the garden's verges—
seeing her new finding— bids, 'My
girl, be not the plant that blushes.
As you grow, be a rose—thorny,
upright, bold, yet with sweet flowers.'

Hibiscus Flower

I like the boom of hibiscus, vivid—
tiny trumpet upon green stalk glossy.
China rose—as it is sometimes called—
is in temple oblation to the deity.

In my boyhood, when I wanted flowers,
hibiscus was my rose, and it was cool
to get its scarlet blooms from frontiers
back on a long walk from my distant school.

And if I hurt my knee while in my play,
I would make, of hibiscus leaves, a paste
to treat me myself, and tired after play,
I would take a drink of hibiscus tart.

In my college, from hibiscus, I learnt
the flower—an array of sepals, petals,
set on the thalamus and the rest of it,
upon a live stalk of a plant species.

Later in life, while watching garden birds,
I kept heeding the small sunbird flutter
alongside the scarlet blooms of hibiscus,
enjoying its little-known sweet nectar.

As I grew up, I owned a piece of land
that had around it a hibiscus fence,
a pruned but tall hedge that kept my land
confined by a long green wall, very nice.

World I saw on that long hibiscus hedge
of creatures many: spiders in gossamer,
squirrels running to trees like on a bridge,
and the tailorbird stitching its quarter.

At dawns, I had a crow-pheasant, a great
fence-sitter with red eyes and the rear bronze.
It would wait for the dawning to be bright
before it jumps to the grass from the fence.

The hibiscus flower is odourless
as it is not keen to blurb its virtues.
Judge not flower by smell since odourless
blooms often beget delicious fruits.

When the Coffee Garden Blooms

At last, when the hills receive rain
after a long winter's dry spell,
blooms en bloc the coffee garden
to rosettes white sweet in smell.

The garden turns into a haven
for honeybees that drone aloft
a fairyland of white and green
rolling upon valleys verdant.

It is when one wakes up to a
coffee garden dawn that one smells
the new bloom that has set to a
magic perfume in night's dark hours.

And then, when one looks at the plants
that has drunk the first rain in greed,
one gets stunned by the new white gems
worn by all of them in great pride.

But the coffee is in a rush
to bear its fruits and so transient
are its new snow-white flowers—blush
they, and in a day or two, wear out.

Past the fragrant white jewel days
soon goes moody, the coffee field,
and it sheds its dead blooms' relics
but finds solace from rain afield.

In weeks, bear green pinhead cherries,
the coffee plants in backup rains.
In months, pinheads grow into berries
holding—in a red pulp—coffee beans.

The cup of coffee that you drain
that makes your day a day—or cheers
you, tired of a hard day—is born
this way in the coffee fields.

SEA

The Sea is an Artist

See, the sea is an artist dexterous.
The swash and the backwater are her tools,
the beach sands primed with water, her canvas,
and the waves her many skilful hands.

Now see, the sea, as backwater backtracks,
leaves a design on the sands: trees, a stand
with buttress roots drilling in sands their tracks.
There swims in swash again, way up the sand.

Now, see, the sea washes off the trees.
It is now a dead sea turtle—swollen
from the sands—that the sea quickly installs
while from the sands, swiftly, the swash swims down.

Now, see, swash swims with a sway from the sea
and seats a sea-urchin on the shingle
up the sand line and quickly shifts the sea
turtle slightly down in an act nimble.

See, a vast swell has emerged in the sea,
like an extended range of bluish hills.
Now, it is way up, reaching a beach tree,
priming the whole beach to a fresh canvas.

A Chat with a Crab on a Riprap

For sure, my crab, you are full of verve.
The way you deal with the tides that strike hard—
keeping your hold on the stones with the nerve
of a lizard on a slick wall—is indeed
incredible; you play with the wave.

Yes, I hear you, my man, from the riprap
as I evade a vast wave from a crack.
There is a cadence in the steady rap
of the sea on the ripraps' pile of rock.
I dodge in sync with that stable flap.

And my man, what you see as red framing
of me is my shroud of the skeleton,
which, I assume, in your case, is hiding
in your flesh. Thus, not feeble, but like stone
is my body to meet the sea's beating.

Fantastic, my crab. What I fancy most
in your response, is the rhythm you said
the sea has when it beats the rocky coast.
It would defeat the best drumroll staged
anywhere with its cadence perfect almost.

My man, I see you not of the riffraff

on the beach who chase crabs on the wet sands,
running after the swash when swells zing off.
See, swell swings onto the stones with debris.
From it, for a morsel, shall I crawl off?

Memories of a Boating in Lakshadweep

Without jerk, was boating across
the lagoon of a coral reef,
but for the old engine's motif—
a grate, a lament crude and coarse.

The gull that escorted the boat
to quite a distance flew its way.
Behind, afar, faded away,
the islet and its palmy coast.

A slender open boat, almost
a canoe was that craft humble,
distant from the mainland's grumble
and now, off the coral isle's coast.

The tranquil waters suddenly
turned turbulent and a hill range—
the Arabian Sea in a rage—
was right in front threateningly.

Two fishermen—one at the rear,
motoring from the stern, another
angling from the bow—together—
cried, 'The sea! Hold onto the bar.'

From the yoke, I leaned to a thwart,

seizing it. The boat skated through
a wave across coral mole. Whew!
The sea! In countless swells athwart.

Up and down, swerving to the right,
and to the left, in jumps and slips,
the warhorse galloped on blue swells,
which screamed, 'See, high seas' might.'

A while later, the chute-the-chute
abruptly ceased, and a calm sea
soothingly sang, 'My dolphins, see…'
Two dolphins arched up in a scoot.

A gull flew low close to the boat.
His—or her—eyes saw no match
on the deck of fish, a catch,
so soon, it left our lone craft.

All blue, all blue, all blue, all blue,
was all way, sans the wake after
the back deck, frothing up astir
and quickly falling back in slew.

Hours down, the tides grew mightier,
and horse's gait from trot to gallop—
up, up, onto the final lap.
A thud, and ho, the breakwater!

The new lagoon said, 'See my shoal
as you drift in,' and palms waved green
flags from the new island, coastline
of which had a red carpet, fish—a school.

A Thousand Seas

Each time I see the blue sea from the shore,
I see a distinct sea with a new design—
a new series of waves that strikes the shore
and over the blue expanse, a new pattern.

Each time bounding waves crash at the shore,
and effervesce to spirals, transient
and the swash swims up the beach ashore,
the crash, beat, froth, bounce and loop are distinct.

Each time the sea raps the riprap barrier
that stands between her and her loved shoreline
she shouts, varying pitch and tone at the bar
that blocks her way to her beloved coastline.

Each time the sea encounters the vast sky,
it's a new horizon—a new formation;
new birds in flight; new shades over the sky;
in the rain, a wet sky; by dusk, a red sun.

Each time I look at life, it's a new life—
new possibilities; chances that wait;
new friendships, a new direction for life.
Hope then wings in, and old griefs abate.

Sunset on Om Beach, Gokarna

Where the cliff in the sea dips fingers,
sketches Om with white sands, the shore.
Where two crescents of Om cohere,
licks waves, the cliff's tongue of boulders.

When downward is the gloaming sun,
golden as gold turns the seaboard.
When the day's last boat from a pod
of dolphins is back, red is the sun.

When the sun paints the sea red, pull
their vessels shoreward, the fishers.
When finally the red sun drowns,
barks the sea at dark rocks spectral.

A Girl Who Sells Lamps on the Beach

The little girl has not seen the golden
glow of gloaming on the Bay of Bengal
dying to darkness over the horizon,
the dark bay's angry rap continual
on the black riprap, the glimmering queue
of bulkhead lamps and the war memorial
overlooking Gandhi's splendid statue.
None of these is for her. She is here to sell.

The trifle she vends dangles from her neck—
crude lamps fashioned from thrown liquor bottles.
Shining battery-backed bulbs that deck
her bottles' bellies glint in many tints.
She is a walking lighthouse. When on dark
corners, seek her light, the promenaders.
Some of them bark inelegantly, 'Heck',
to her presence, though none she pesters.

As the dusk grows old, throng the cobbled walk
of the beach, seeking the bay's soothing breeze,
travellers and Puducherry's townsfolk.
Where narrow strips of muddy sand lace
one end of the riprap and whirling waves,
like a path to French India, an old bridge—
on slender limbs onto the dark bay—limps.

The little seller sees no bay or bridge.

She sees no lit joints where kids enjoy
ice cream or the ancient unlit lighthouse.
She—a lighted lighthouse—lights her way
like a walking stall. She has no issue
with any moody walker who, on her
footfall, might grunt in deep displeasure.
Grins Mickey Mouse, from a bill, at her.
Tired, she sinks below Gandhi's statue.

Impression

Printing my footprints on the beach,
alone, I am afoot to reach
where the sea is in endless preach.

Far back, my long walk began
on the beach sand where lofty pine
trees, like a wall, stand in a line.

I shuffled on, pulling out my
feet from mats of loose sand, dry,
printing deep holes as I passed by.

Ahead, on somewhat hard soil—
less sandy—I impressed my sole—
a flatfish with each footfall.

Now, on a course, wet and hard,
where, from shallow pits, crabs guard
the sea, I make no more tread.

I end my lonely walk here.
I've no more impression where
sea sermons to me and the shore.

MAN

Alzheimer's Disease

As I realise my failing memory
that I sometimes forget that I had my
morning tea, and I had my daily pills
I know it is time that I pen my thoughts.

Memory! How many times in the past
I badly wanted an exit from it,
when it prickled me with moments dismal
of frustration, rejection, and denial!

Memory! How many times in the past
I fancied it to be picky about
bringing forth in mind fortunate moments
of content, selection, and acceptance!

Now! With a sigh, I say not a sieve
is memory; it's a transparent pane
passing shafts of light—moments of life past.
When mildew hazes glass, subdued is light.

I wonder how I can still write these lines
in a tongue, I love, of my deep feelings—
a faculty, I know, will soon fade away
like an ephemeral bloom falls to decay.

I may, one day, forget this pen and take
it for my toothbrush, and then when I seek
the tap walking to my couch, will you hold
me and get my brush, or become a scold?

Life, as I know it now, is not just
living but recalling, too, one's days past.
And when it shrinks to chores, mundane
life is just things past in reflection.

As long as I remember my moments
past and perceive the ongoing struggles
I'm alive; I die when memory dies.
I shall then be akin to a corpse.

Oh! What did I speak about, my love?
Or were you talking about the dove
that coos lowly from the mango tree?
Why haven't you given me a cup of tea?

A Deathbed Thought

Why do you wear that worried stare
as I lie here waiting for death?
A smile on your lips would be fair.

I know what does your stare bear
as your eyes scan me all my length.
Why do you wear that worried stare?

Of your wonder, I am aware—
Your name my memory still hath?
A smile on your lips would be fair.

Know this—my mind still has a glare,
but my lips fail, though I have breath.
Why do you wear that worried stare?

I've many things spoken, nowhere,
although from me, no word now cometh.
A smile on your lips would be fair.

All my life, dear to me, you were.
Stay glad always, you, wish I doth.
Why do you wear that worried stare?
A smile on your lips would be fair.

That Moment

All that I remember of that moment
is that I was driving a car, and it
went astray, giving me a fleeting sight
of a big tree across a blaring blast.

As though winged, I rose high up in the sky
and saw men rushing down that motorway
to where the car, in flattened metal, lay
in a pool of blood like a huge, crushed fly.

I saw my body for just an instant—
a work of art done on metal, abstract—
as I soared high and high, very distant
from the world on that lonely, rapid flight.

All I know now of myself is that
I am a ray of light of a flux, bright.
Beyond this, of things else too blank, I am.
How can I with no brain and engram?

Creator

She had been working for several days
on that painting of Christ's head slantwise
on the cross. At first, she painted a cross
but rubbed it away from the canvas.

'Only the face in pain on sharp focus.'
Sketching a face, she worked on it, agony,
the Passion on the cross at Calvary—
convulsing flesh, rolling eyes, gaping jaws.

Bringing to mind how the soldiers at Skull,
the site of the scene of her work, mocked Jesus,
she worked out a wreath of thorns on the tress.
'Recall me when in thy power, royal.'

And advanced thus, at last, the work of art
reached its finish, and from a distance, she
reviewed it—'What went amiss, I shall see
later,' and left her frame—final not yet.

After a few days, she came to the easel
that had Passion, which she had depicted.
A fresh pair of eyes saw what was needed
to complete the work still on the easel.

She squeezed out a blob of blood-red pigment
and applied it as stains of blood down where
the crown of thorns touched the temple and err
she did not in strokes and said, 'It's complete.'

At that moment, when at the art she looked,
she felt her eyes swell up, and hands shiver.
She fell to her knees and, with a quiver,
'My Lord, my God,' she broke into cries, awed.

Brain and Mind

Wise is the man who listens to the brain.
He knows how round is this world's ways.
No straight path leads one to temporal gain.
No cat chases its prey on a straight trace.

A person wise always eludes the poem
because it may get him on the wrong track.
He knows it is better to click a modem
to see the trend in the market of stock.

The thought in any choice of the wise
is not the concern for others but bread.
Are there big cats in forests with kind eyes
so teary when a fawn limps in a herd?

Yet not, unwise, yet not, the man who heeds
the mind; ever begets joy, his kind deeds.

Fifth Candle

'Advent wreath from evergreen sheaves,'
chanted she, before what she made,
'of candles five on deep green leaves.'

One rose and three purple candles
around a white candle adorned
advent wreath from evergreen sheaves.

On Sunday one, one of the purples,
she, in purples and prayers, kindled,
of candles five on deep green leaves.

With two more purples, she, in purples,
on the next two Sundays kindled,
advent wreath from evergreen sheaves.

On Sunday four, she, in roses,
the rose one, through carols kindled,
of candles five on deep green leaves.

On Christmas day, she lit, in whites,
the candle white, and her eyes flamed,
advent wreath from evergreen sheaves,
of candles five on deep green leaves.

Two Brothers on a Swing

I spent that night in a hospital foyer,
staying awake around the night
as the bystander for a patient
in critical care, my brother.

As night advanced, fell to silence
the hall, but for a clock in a tick,
the mosquitoes in a droning talk,
the ceiling fans' whir in cadence.

Spoke of the time that dies, the clock;
of blood and beats of heart, the flies;
of breath and lungs, the leaves of fans;
of the midnight hour, the clock's stroke.

Another day, my nightmare did find.
I recalled my brother's sad gaze
at me for a wink through pain ablaze
last when in senses was his mind.

And then, a call came to my phone.
'Fast to the intensive care,' said
a voice, and I dashed through a dread
to a stark truth to be thrown.

I saw the graph plummeting flat
and digits to zero in the fall.
To a time very distant, I fell—
two brothers on a swing in a flight.

Onboard is General

(Remembering Bipin Rawat, India's top General who died in a helicopter crash in the Nilgiris)

Go whirl and whirl, you whirlybird.
Onboard is our beloved General.
Up and up soar you, metal bird.

Do slice the skies, empyreal,
but do that on a high alert.
On thy ways are hills several.

You might fly by many a turret
of mountain ranges very steep
attired in their verdant tree skirt.

Confront you might mist in a leap,
like a thousand palls in the wind.
Bypass it; evade its hard sweep.

Heavy rainfall might make you blind,
that being the style in the hills.
Do bear all these in thy bird mind.

And give not the General the chills.

Christmas Night

Light, it is Christmas light.
Tonight is going long.
Night, this is Christmas night.

All are in great delight.
Trees hold stars all along.
Light, it is Christmas light.

Dew falls early tonight.
Aloud, the church bells bong.
Night, this is Christmas night.

Children sing by firelight,
a graceful Carol song.
Light, it is Christmas light.

Santa, in the limelight,
dances to a ding-dong.
Night, this is Christmas night.

Merry words are in flight—
'Peace and goodwill, lifelong!'
Light, it is Christmas light.
Night, this is Christmas night.

The Last Day in Office

It was another day for the babus
of that government office, higher.
And as usual, they indulged in rounds
of gossip, gab, and noting in that order.
Files moved up and down with queries
and in and out missives transited,
with enclosures of demands and reports
with that banal day date-stamped.

Yet, for the head of that office, it meant
a distinct day, although he sat cabined
as usual, to notes signing his consent
in files classified urgent, red-flagged.
His assistant had strict instructions that
he wanted no visitors and no one,
on the telephone—unless so urgent—
since the last day of duty, he was on.

He had a small mirror, which he had long
forgotten in his drawer, which that day
with his personal effects came along
to his hands as he, on that final day
gathered his few items of possession.
He looked into the mirror with interest
and felt he saw his ghost in reflection—

from the first day of service—he a ghost.

It's not just his last day in that office
but of his long service, the final day.
He spoke in farewell to the office
when it was time to wind up that last day.
Soon, an assistant held to him a report.
He relieved himself of charge, signing it.
Sadly, then, he broke his pen's nib that
wrote all these years his order and note.

When, at last, he came out of his cabin
to walk the life left, up the office stood,
hands in namaste, and slowly then,
saying no to the office car, he dropped
down the stairway. And beyond the garden
that for several long years, he heeded,
on another journey—unaided, alone—,
he joined the street and melted in the crowd.

Toddy Tapper

Look at this Palmyra palm with a hale
dusky trunk with many ring-like leaf scars,
a crown of massive fan-like greenish fronds,
and blooms a long bunch—like a ponytail.

Look at the stumps of limbs on a bamboo pole,
rungs of a primal ladder bound tightly
with a firm rope of coir to the scary,
sturdy, towering Palmyra palm bole.

Look at an earthen pot sienna dangled
from the yellow ponytail, an urn for
the sap dripping of blooms myriad tender
tapped earlier with a cutter, sharp-edged.

Look at the beaten mud alley, betwixt
trees and over an outcrop of swarming
thorns reaching the Palmyra palm winding,
a tricky passage for anyone through it.

Look at the lone lean man—but quite sturdy,
draped in a loud cloth about his middle
and with a bare chest and shanks—in amble,
shod with slippers on the thorny alley.

Look at the way he reaches the tall palm,
trilling like a warbler, a song's few lines,
one from a film, and as the morn sun hits
him in eyes, he hoods his eyes with a palm.

Look at how he scales the bamboo ladder,
keeping close to it, his body brunet,
lifting his eyes to the dangling clay pot,
singing still, despite his climbing ladder.

Look at how nicely he unties the urn,
drooping it on his shoulder and dropping
through the Palmyra pronto, not spilling
the palm wine, singing once again a tune.

Pearl Anniversary

'Say,' she sang, 'say, something about thirty.'
'To two times three times five, it is equal;
a square pyramidal number is thirty,
it, being the first four squares in total.'

'No maths. Consider something else,' she said.
'Then,' he piped, 'thirty days has September….'
'No! Too late! I am not a preschool ward,
to learn months, April, June and November.'

'Then, Judas and pieces of silver, thirty…'
'Oh no! That is a tale of disloyalty.'
'Well, then, at years of age, about thirty…'
'I know; Jesus started his ministry.'

'Something else? Well, number thirty sonnet:
'When to the sessions of sweet silent thought,
 I summon up remembrance of things past…'
'The Bard! But I lack not anything I sought!'

'My, my! My, my! Pearl anniversary!'
'But you forgot that and for me a gift.'
'Forgot? Pearl for pearl anniversary,
and lily as a rich floral tribute.'

'No gemstone, white lily is fine; piety
and purity. Yet, I want, beyond symbols…'
'What would be that?' He fell into anxiety.
With a sob, she said, 'Thirty more years.'

Wake

An elderly merchant of high esteem
lay supine in his usual bright whites.
He somehow hid a smile and spoke no words.
He was dead; it was the wake in his home.

A horde of people viewed him with flowers
and offered prayers whispered in grief, hushed,
as into the wake, incense wafted
from benzoin gum sticks burnt in bunches.

Sat there teary, the dead man's kin, reading
aloud from a book, prayers for the dead—
often snivelling its lines, distressed,
and at times, watching viewers passing.

A cross—witness to the vigil—stood,
sandwiched between candles burning—a pair—
beside a casket, placed on a bier
that was the dead man's last bed.

Then, it was time for a minister to rise,
with words visiting the life of the dead
and prayer in verses sounding sad.
On a sad note, ended, the service.

To the hearse, bearers lifted the pall,
 kinfolk raised a lament and started
on a dirge, his last trip, the departed—
'Bye, home; let me leave the world, temporal…'

The cortege passed with dirges, past shops,
on town roads that stayed closed in farewell
to the merchant onto fields asphodel
from his worldly life of commodities.

Smell the Roses

Stop and smell the roses, won't you?
Life is very short, as you know.
As you give work, give life its due.
Stop and smell the roses, won't you?
When did you last see the sea blue?
Over the green hills drifting snow?
Stop and smell the roses, won't you?
Life is very short, as you know.

Adieu, Alma Mater

Alone under an ancient tree, I was
watching the campus keenly, and it was
silent on that Sunday, and its lovely
pebbled winding walkways, very lonely.

I heard a koel singing and felt its
melody gloomy as it repeated its
single note to a crescendo gracious,
before ending it in abrupt quietus.

I heard a dove cooing from a dark nook
of the majestic building of red brick,
where I had decades ago my classes
by great teachers for several long years.

I heard mynas, a big flock, landing on
the green grasses, where they gaily hopped on,
their heads in lively chatter, bobbing,
like a gang of classmates, revelling.

I heard soughing upon branches, a wind
shaking upon me many dry leaves, dead.
I looked up and saw plenty of fresh leaves,
green and youthful, on tender twigs.

I had this converse as I left the tree:
Remember, do you, grand tree, this oldie,
who loved on days youthful, thy shade, soothing,
and who missed no day under you, dreaming?

I heard the koel resuming its song
behind me—the same dismal note rising.
I may not come again, alma mater.
Let new dreams ever bloom here, ever.

Eternity

'From my rotting body, flowers shall grow,
and I am in them, and that is eternity.'
- Edvard Munch

The sun was just up, and the dawn half-dark
when, alone, I stood by that grave, gloomy.
Lost forever to a sad memory
rested a buddy inside in the dark.

I saw by the side of the tomb a plant
bearing teeny scarlet flowers, dewed,
like to the soul of my departed friend,
where the earth took him, a live tribute.

From that bush, I plucked stalks, flowery,
and as a bouquet, offered them over
the melancholy grave with a prayer
and sank in thoughts of death's mystery.

'O, friend, as flowers I grow from my tomb.'
I heard a low voice, disembodied.
'That is eternity, blooms from the dead.'
'It's my tear, not dew, you see on the bloom.'

Onam

'Twas on a stubble field of rice,
that boys with baskets full of blooms
freshly plucked from endemic herbs
ran with delight at a slow pace.

'Twas upon a quaint little yard
of a house with a tiled roof that girls
rapidly flew on swings from boughs
of mango trees, tall and splendid.

'Twas next to blooms afresh from fields,
and laid to a pattern in a yard
that with loud and rhythmic claps, whirled,
in charming steps, flowery girls.

'Twas on a street of milling folk
that I beheld men—potbellied
and as fierce tigers painted—
dancing in costumes, bespoke.

'Twas in a passing parade down
a green village path where I saw
ambling a portly king below
a brolly of dry palm leaf brown.

'Twas on a roughcast floor inside
a village house, where sat to a feast
served on the plantain leaf plate
with fun and frolic a household.

'Twas then from my sleep I awoke
—breaking the lovely dream I had—
to a vehicle's sound in the yard—
a delivery van's low honk.

'Twas Onam day and I overslept.
The mall's van delivered me wrapped
in plastic and securely boxed
what I had pre-booked—Onam's feast.

First Death Anniversary

The wheel of time rolls on and on and on,
ticking, ticking, ticking; the year is flawed,
a unit for time's pace on its motion
to eternity; yet, like a child, friend,
I count the waves that make an ocean.
It is now one year since you left untold
to the Elysian Fields to dwell unknown.

O, Darling Baby, Sleep

O, darling baby, sleep.
It's night, too dull and dark.
To lovely dreams, you sweep.

Stare not in darkness, deep.
No soul sits in the park.
O, darling baby, sleep.

The fireflies are asleep,
and no dog sends a bark.
To lovely dreams, you sweep.

Deep in sleep is black sheep.
The moo-cow's snore, you hark.
O, darling baby, sleep.

Of cars, roads have no beep.
At night shall sing no lark.
To lovely dreams, you sweep.

At dawn, you play bo-peep,
waking up when birds chirp.
O, darling baby, sleep.
To lovely dreams, you sweep.

Ruins of Vijayanagar

As I rose on stairs to a stage, ancient—
a neat stack of chiselled stones of granite—
figures in relief stared coldly at me
from a dead empire and medieval time:
elephants in a march; sporting hats, envoys;
on horseback, soldiers; in dance, girls;
one-humped camels bearing drummers;
slaying a fearsome bear, many warriors.

Growing to twilight was eventide,
atop that old podium as I stood.
From there, long back, the sovereign
watched the Navaratri celebration.
What once had the name Vijayanagar,
the capital city of an empire
lay there around me in countless ruins,
in a vast, desolate land of silence.

I watched the eerie dry terrain as far
as the horizon, spiked by hills of tor—
basement skeletons of a city lost;
relics of courts wrecked in a holocaust;
lost homes of nobles who conspired
against the emperor who once governed
the length and breadth of South India;

trails of streets and markets of a lost era.

Afar, along boulders, a river flowed
invisible to me from where I stood—
a stream where once bathed elephants
that fought combats to conquests
till in the battle of Talikota,
fell the empire into absolute rot,
ruins of which lay before me, scattered
like tombs in a melancholic graveyard.

From afar, I heard the clunk of a bell,
maybe from the Virupaksha temple,
where cohorts worshipped their God.
The city fell, but this temple survived
the cataclysm and pillage, relentless.
Above decayed, crownless coconut trees
that stood like sentinels of the ruin
crows flew and sunk to the tors, the sun.

New Year's Day

Burns down the dead year
in the eastern sky's pyre
to a blue glow and falls
as ashes to the hills.

Kindles the new-born year,
the sun; the sky in fear
blanches above the hill
but soon twinkles in thrill.

Awaken the sleeping trees.
Songbirds out in the breeze
warble in a pleased voice—
It's the new year; rejoice.

To My Hilltop Hut in a Dusk

Half-dead was the winter day when I hit
the foot of the hill and on a lonesome
hill trail, as I hiked to my hilltop hut,
junglefowl sent a roosting call, winsome.

With birds roosting, but for a gentle breeze
that winnowed fuzzes of floating mist,
the jungle pathway and the stands of trees—
hazy apparitions—were silent.

Bower yonder hindered me—a tusker,
a boar gored pronto into the silence.
Trust me; it chose not to be a thruster
but tore into the scrub sans violence.

A gully feebly sobbed like a low lass,
her rockface sad and teary, with dirges
dismal were her visitor cicadas,
and her frills of bamboo in wild surges.

Too old, the twilight was in death throes
when, in a clearing, my slog saw its end.
My little yard had seen no broom for days,
so I had to flog the weeds on the sod.

When I shoved the foredoor of my hut,
from a limb of a jack tree, a scops-owl
had an interrogative hoot—'What?'
Up came the full moon, the night sky's smile.

Missed Flowers

Last night, I had a long dream, an odd one.
Whose, I know not, but it was a mandate.
It required me to descend a mountain,
alone and along a trail desolate.

I had to set out at the crack of dawn
down a rugged, devious, hilly track
and reach the plains below by sundown
taking just one break for rest on the trek.

At first, I shuffled through a precipice.
The slope then turned grassy and flowery.
Flowers, one by one, told me, 'Fragrance!
Smell me for it; halt in this lap, bowery.'

'No,' I said, 'I got to get on,' and sped
away like a flushed boar, leaving the blooms
and down and down and down I rashly hiked
my hard way through weeds and legumes.

Farther down, many trees offered me fruits.
'No,' I said, 'I got to get on,' and sped.
Then I saw the path dry, empty of plants,
and under the hot sun, dead tired, I trod.

On the hill's foot, I approached the plane
of thorny brushwood by late evening.
Panting and sweating, I sank to a stone,
availing my break well before gloaming.

As I rested, a spiny scrub stung me.
I rued that I missed many a flower.
I craved to smell a bloom and eat a berry,
but saw only thorns and my ebbing hour.

The Night Before My Wedding

Why is tonight so bright and so starry?
Whence the sky picked, jewels very shiny?
Why is a lone star brighter and glary?

Why am I, wonder I, not yet weary,
jaywalking night sky's gemstones, so tiny?
Why is tonight so bright and so starry?

Why is, tonight, my heart very cheery,
leaping skyward with joy in agony?
Why is a lone star brighter and glary?

Does the wind, for me, the fragrance carry
of jasmine vine, bearing blossoms sheeny?
Why is tonight so bright and so starry?

Why is the owlet quiet and not scary
while the koels pitch up in harmony?
Why is a lone star brighter and glary?

Am I all eyes for the new moon, deary,
for whom the stars are fireworks uncanny?
Why is tonight so bright and so starry?
Why is a lone star brighter and glary?

When I Died

From my lifeless body, I rose skyward.
Far down, briefly, I saw wailing kinfolk.
As a feather, pronto, I soared upward.

Shortly, I lost sight of the verdant land
into the clouds as I soared like a lark.
From my lifeless body, I rose skyward.

I never again thought of the world,
its pricking thorns or my painful years, dark.
As a feather, pronto, I soared upward.

I wonder whether it's true that I died.
It was birth, a liberation stark.
From my lifeless body, I rose skyward.

As I flew in the sky, I rejoiced.
Misery was my worldly life's hallmark.
As a feather, pronto, I soared upward.

Far up and farther than the sun, I soared
until I joined a bright light as a spark.
From my lifeless body, I rose skyward.
As a feather, pronto, I soared upward.

War

Hark! Afar firearms are in a fierce fire.
Abandoned by the dawn birds is the sky.
Surges to a bus bay townsfolk off an alley.
Sirens in a cops' cab; close is danger.
Feeling looming doom in the lengthy bay
is a forsaken dog, left with no ray
of hope of joining its lost master.

Bending on a baby girl, her father
fixes her bobble hat, which is awry.
To his heart, up he lifts her with a sigh.
'Smile, my baby,' he whispers, 'soldier
is your daddy, so don't be teary
but be happy, jolly with thy mummy,
and play and play all day in the bunker.
After the war, for you, baby, Daddy
shall get a dolly and a good toffee.
Board fast; the bus leaves for the shelter.'
Planting a kiss on her cheek, rosy,
he lifts her to her mother— now weepy—,
fighting tears down his cheek, the fighter.

Live in the Present

Live in the present and its great pleasures.
From dawning to gloaming, enjoy today.
Every wink dies in the next, and the day
in the next, so precious are all moments.

A bird lives that way—short is its life span.
The koel has not a day for sad notes
and the next and the next for joyful notes.
It has the same warble time and again.

No thrush sings in melancholy mode
one dawning—fit for a bleak notation—
and gladly, the following: to the dawn
sun every day thrush has the same ode.

The past is 'was', and the future a 'may.'
The present is 'is', and it holds treasures.
Live in the present and its great pleasures.
From dawning to gloaming, enjoy today.

Deaddiction Ward

'Hoo! Hoo!' It's in delirium, a shout
from a man tied to the bedstead, a frog
in an anatomy lab tacked to mount.

'This is hell. Why do you, like a fox, howl?'
asks a nurse while pricking the man's finger.
A medic arrives almost in a prowl.

'Disoriented, yet,' says the doctor.
'Man, can you specify this place and me?'
Quickly comes the reply, 'Bar and bartender.'

Sundays

The distant peal of church bell, tolling folks
from a lazy day to hymns of glory,
church-walking laity in finery,
silent noontide when owlets sit on boughs,
noisy dusk of gatherings gaily,
an agile mongoose on a quiet pathway
stalking slithering snakes in stunted shrubs,
a rush of urchins on even clearings
howling all the while with a ball rolling,
for her master, a tethered cow lowing:
All these in the dead past made my Sundays.

Polling Booth

The queue of voters slithers like a snake,
tail still in the yard of the polling booth.
The morn stays lovely from the daybreak.

Past the checks that found everything fine
to smooth onset rolls on the poll when
to a mumble shrink the talks in the line.

A crow lands on a guava in the yard.
Clueless about the queue, it keeps looking
for a child eating a loaf in the quad.

Finding none, it appraises guava fruits.
Selecting the best, it enjoys its pick,
and caws, 'always elect the very best.'

In a Bar Near Our lady of Good Health

He was in a hurry in the bar,
a bracelet-wearing dandy.
He ordered two pegs of brandy
and yelled, 'And two eggs, waiter.'

The swell shivered with fury
when the drinks came without eggs.
He shouted at the server, 'Eggs?'
Draining a glass, he screamed, 'Hurry!'

Through the second glass, now empty,
stared at the tender, the fellow
when the eggs came pronto.
'Repeat: two eggs and two brandy.'

Past his order roared, the macaroni—
'Waiter, as you are a shirker,
I am yet with the starter.
Oh, I'll be late at Our Lady.'

As the Earth Takes Her

And now, tomb slabs cover the burial
and stay adorned with wreaths from the vigil.
The earth has just taken an old lady.
Grievers are gone, and dismal dirges die.

One man stays, squatting sadly on the floor,
his dejected gaze on the blooms galore
in an ample heap upon the grave slabs
alone beneath which, in peace, his wife sleeps.

Sank in sorrow, he invokes the red rose
that he, on their wedding day, for her, chose,
and the smile with which she slowly with it
adorned her braid of hair like a gem fit.

Too aged, childless, and now a widower,
he senses that, in a way, it's better
that his wife, before him, went to the grave
for her grief, he cannot bear in his grave.

Retrospect of a Retiree

Retirees at the reunion had the same
long tongue when each recounted how a boar—
a grunter with tapered tusks—sometimes came
to strike each and how each fled with a roar.

One modest man levelled a serious blame
on a cunning boar that often stalked him to gore.
One day, it struck him from his back and made him lame
for two years, and he found it very hard to bear.

Finding it stupid to be backstabbers' aim,
he left his work in that wilderness forever.
The retirees lamented, 'On that shrewd boar shame.'
A while stayed at the reunion, that whimper.

Post-op

Asleep, I was way down in an abyss.
Fetching my senses, I heard a voice.
It called out my name, my name, and I rose.
From death-like darkness, I, I rose, I rose.

I blinked at the light where figures silhouetted.
Past a green gown, my eyes slowly focussed
on a medic's mutter, 'Done, stay composed.'
and the web of tubes that held me restrained.

My hungry eyes jaywalked the post-op care,
pierced a transparent pane and fell
on a twig in the yard on a bright bole,
bobbing in the breeze, a lovely flower.

The Wanderer in the Town

Messy hair, tattered clothes, face unshaven,
a long beard like a mop stuck on the chin,
a blank stare—that was that nomadic man,
maybe in his thirties—with a smile, wan.

Sporadic was his sighting in the town.
He would suddenly pop on any lane,
the beach, the bus stand or the fish market.
He was sober and never posed a threat.

For donation, he pestered nobody.
In a downtown churchyard, on a Sunday,
with a fistful of dust, he said deadpan,
like a thinker, 'This dust was once the man.'

Another time, in the park, he, to a rose,
sang, 'O, my love is like a red, red rose.'
Once on the beachfront, in a voice, sad,
he said, 'I wandered lonely as a cloud.'

'Whitman, Burns, and Wordsworth; very worthy
is this dude,' said a read lad, 'Newsworthy.'
But when the hip lad found it, the nomad
was already gone as a roving cloud.

No one noticed him again on the beach,
park, or market or heard his sorry speech.
But now the town's boys often hum Burns,
'O, my love is like a red, red rose.'

Drink Responsibly

That was a red flag, a diagnosis.
In his game, he saw waiting, a danger—
responsible drinking or cirrhosis.
He has been a meandering river
of alcohol for several seasons.
But for him, the game was not yet over.
He began to glance—not after glasses—
the gloaming sun's ineffable grandeur,
and flocks back to roost on distant trees.

He started rising early in the dawn
to watch the dawn beading dew on the rose,
eastern hills smiling to the sun new-born,
in two minds, cuckoo sitting on the fence,
babbling babblers probing the verdant lawn,
and on the step, the house cat's lazy doze.
He found his new lifeworld in the mundane
everyday scenes, and that gave him bliss.

Birth of a Poem

Closeted away with my pen, I mused
over a plot for another poem,
but it did not work out, and so bemused,
I invoked Muse for a theme and rhyme.

Muse said, 'Go for a long walk, a long walk.'
And thus, I saw myself afoot afield.
Passing beside a pond, I found ducks quack
and quack at a buffalo, by him spooked.

A purple heron was upon a bog.
It stretched its neck like a stick by the reeds.
Was it a neck or a snake stalking a frog?
Reading my mind, it bowed its neck like 's'.

I eyed a lad homeward prodding a cow,
often turning to turn its tail slightly.
Lowing a low low, slowly ploughed the cow,
baulking by blades, bulging its tongue lightly.

'Alliteration!' Muse whispered to me,
'This is how you walk over a poem.
Muse over the mundane; feel what you see.
When emotions prick, the mind bleeds poem.'

Walking Beside a Marsh

A bog beside a lea with scenes charmed me
when I took a morning stroll on the lea.

The wings of a pond heron became white
when the grey bird skyward rose in a flight.

A sleep-prone buffalo dropped to the ground
stealing a few more quick winks in the mud.

From the marshland, wavered its slender neck
like a slithering snake, a darter, black.

Rose from rest, seeing me, a dog, a stray,
wagging its tail, wishing me a great day.

The sun, a red smear far above the marsh,
was very mellow and not at all harsh.

The bog and the lea made my day this way.
Things workaday often make the man's day.

Retirement Wishes

Gardner, each plant you planted and tended
hold blooms—in gratitude for you, indeed—
as you leave for good today with a sigh,
in pridefulness, your head held very high.

Every plant knows how, through rain and shine,
you, from the seed, raised it in the garden.
For long years, you did miss the rising sun
and the deep red horizon of sundown.

Retired and home, you keep a small garden
of roses, lilies, and vines of jasmine.
Be there every dawn, harking the chorus
of happy birds and rapid bee flight's buzz.

Retire, o, gardener, to thy life's new dawn.
Retire, gardener, to thy life, a garden,
still verdant, fragrant and ever-blooming,
and live thy peaceful day till it's gloaming.

The Day We Left the Village

The day we left the village for the town
bag and baggage is a faded memory.
I find, lost in time's forgotten bylane,
myself, back then, yet a tiny schoolboy.

All I recall of it is a wheeler
that left the hamlet with a stack of sacks,
my parents, my siblings, me, and our
old dog that sat bobbing from the packs.

Now, decades down, as an older man,
for the first time after that translocation
I am in a car, passing by the green
remote hamlet, once our habitation.

The old winding earthen pathway is now
a broad, straight, even, blackish macadam
with no ox-drawn cart or jaywalking cow.
On its silent verges stand stunning homes.

The fields, then vast paddies, are now empty
of the crop of any grain and oxen
draft nowhere a plough and plods in muddy
wakes, prodding a weary yoke, no ploughman.

And now I pull up my car by a stand
of tall coconut palms, our old homestead.
There, I see a dwelling, modern and grand;
its porch stands where we had cattle shed.

Down memory lane, I drift as a plume.
In a verdant grove of palm and plantain,
a boy urges a cow taller than him,
often twisting her tail, braving a rain.

A Gravestone Triolet

Memento mori, memento mori,
o, beholder, whisper this from thy heart.
In dust shall end thy life of vainglory.
Memento mori, memento mori.
To sleep in death's dark, undying valley
of eternal silence, thou shall depart.
Memento mori, memento mori,
o, beholder, whisper this from thy heart.

A Time Seen with Ears

The coronavirus contagion
downed my town onto a rigid lockdown.
Then, like others, I mainly stayed indoors,
and my ears were my eyes on life outdoors.

I would hear the avenue—a course mute
but for many ambulances en route
to hospitals and the jeeps of police
dashing away at a frightening pace.

Buildings blinded my view of the main road,
but I could make out which vehicle wailed
and which sent out a blaring siren rude—
one a lament, the other a command.

From the minaret, the muezzin's loud call,
I would feel a cry to all faiths to fall
to knees in devotion—o, God, the town,
the virus pandemic is out to down.

In the neighbourhood, the techies working
from home spoke aloud on headphones, coding,
bugged by their screaming kiddies, denied
play in the park, although the school stayed closed.

From the trees, even in the hot noontide,
sang to the lockdown, a lyrical ode
unfamiliar birds from distant forests
exploring the locked township like tourists.

Silent was not the town—although in dread—
in with the sick and out with the dead
when ambulances wailed on days of tears
of the pandemic—a time seen with ears.

Meadow's Morning Walkers

Flashes through fleecy clouds deep red a sun
as walkers tread the lea, awash in dew.
In sweet trills, a drongo, as though for fun
skyward bobs its head, greeting the dawn new.

A man walks a content dog that keeps taut
its leash all the way, often swerving to sniff
at the grass, and at times, taking a bite
quick of it, ripping the blades with a whiff.

A pack of stray dogs, jealous of the pet
dog's privilege, yaps from a distance, safe,
its despair, and the scrub echoes that threat
for a long while, much to the walkers' chafe.

An elderly lady throws her hands like
paddles from a canoe and propels her
stocky person across the meadow, like
on a rough road, a jerky jeep, astir.

A bevy of lassies pads the grassland,
chatting and erupting into giggles,
and on its tail, a teeny-weeny child
exerts to keep step in rapid scuttles.

Down on a reedy swamp, from sticky silt,
rises a water buffalo to plod
when on its hump lands, a cattle egret
for a bumpy ride through the marshy sod.

Far up, the sun, now white but very bright,
begins athwart the sky, its rapid hike.
The walkers on the lea are now replete
with the glow of heaven's light in the strike.

Pepper Pickers of Malabar

In Malabar, a pepper field has coral trees
as standards, and the frail pepper vines
entwining them are like loose overalls
draping their thorny boles in deep greens.

The grower maintains coral trees with crowns
cut very thin, and thus, the pepper vines
get a balanced shade and sunshine— always
for their timely flowering after rains.

I say this, pausing to see a farmer
reap his berries on a bamboo ladder.
It only dawned when the pepper grower
walked in, bearing on his shoulder a ladder.

Through the unipolar bamboo ladder,
pronto to many metres, the farmer
clambers a prickly standard that bears
a vine with berry-bearing spikes galore.

His unstable foot on the ladder dreads
him not as he plucks ripe pendulous spikes,
stretching himself on the bower, his hands
deftly combing the straggling vine for drupes.

The plucked spikes go straight to a fabric sack
secured like a pouch on the farmer's back—
upon the coral tree, his crude backpack
that oft to and fro dangles on his back.

The slack sack slowly swells like a belly
burdened by the harvested berry
and so, the farmer dips in a hurry
and drops the crop in a bag of gunny.

To another vine, when the farmer walks,
I glimpse on a yonder vine, scarlet eyes
of koels—infamous berry-lifters—
secretly cherry-picking red berries.

Loneliness

Alone and in life's darkening twilight,
I often noticed myself in distress
and my mind winging on an awful fright.
Loneliness was my problem, I confess.

I yearned to slay that terrible demon,
that like a rodent gnawed my happiness,
the awareness of being all alone.
Cognition often breeds unhappiness.

Then, one day, I saw a sweet little bird
with many an adorable feather
that from my neighbour's garden warbled
a tune melodious beyond measure.

What makes you so happy, lone little bird?
Shall you teach me your sweet musical tune?
Visit my yard, too, to sing what I heard—
One may be alone, but still not alone.

Where will the bird sit to sing in my yard?
My yard hosts only a few straggling weeds.
So, I started planting in my dooryard
an array of bushes and tree saplings.

What a pleasure watching the bushes grow.
Watering them at dawning and tending
them, seeing, from sprouts, they slowly grow
is letting them live with nature blending.

Bulbuls were the first visitors flying
into my new garden, flicking their heads
thoughtfully on every plant, inspecting
each one closely and trilling in gladness.

Then magpie robins arrived, jerking
their tiny tails, with pleasing notes, drongoes,
parrots with rose necklaces feasting
on the first fruits of young guava trees.

To the chorus of birds, every dawning
I pad the yard these days and, on the lawns,
often, I notice, behind me, chatting
a hunting flock of yellow-billed babblers.

A bird taught me how not to be alone.
Nature has a song, but one must listen
to the sound of the birds, wind, sea and rain.
One may be alone, but still not alone.

The Boy Who Walked to the Skies

(Rock Stars: Babu hung in there,
Indian Army heroes did the rest-
The Times of India, Kochi, February 10, 2022)

The boy knew not that the peak falls
where it almost abuts the skies.
The boy who liked a walk to the skies,
hiked and hiked to the skies, he hiked.

Where the peak fell, the boy, too, fell
off a sheer rockface in a hard fall.
The boy, on his skywalk, sadly fell
and flew in a chute of black rock.

But in a faultline, he got stuck
below the head of the high peak.
Thus, the boy hiker sadly stuck,
sticking to the high rock all day.

In the night, in the notch so high,
the boy heard the cliff, 'In the sky,
you are; now see the stars, my boy,
until abseils to you, an angel.'

Candid Snapshots of Life

The mind has a camera shooting candids.
It takes shots of things and deeds, mundane.
A slideshow of these chance images aids
to render the profile of life genuine.

Recall that night long ago when the moon
was merely a narrow waxing crescent,
and you and I stood by the sea on a dune
barked at by the sea in rage, incessant.

Once, you and I were on a long highway,
running out of cash, driving our old car.
Low was our fuel tank on that long way,
and we drank water to quench our hunger.

Long ago, you and I scoured a streamside
looking for the songster bird in the brush
that sang a long-winded tune from the wild
and we found it was a whistling thrush.

Remember, you and I cried in the rain
unseen by anybody when we fell
bleeding badly on life's outcrop of thorn.
Recollect, you said rain has a tear smell.

A hug, a smile, a teardrop, and a deed
heedful are usual frames the mind clicks
for the scrapbook of man's life, and indeed
mind's candid images are life's landmarks.